GRADUATE EMPLOYABILITY: CAN HIGHE

Angela Maher and Sarah Graves

Graduate Employability
Can higher education deliver?

Threshold Press

First published 2008 by
Threshold Press Ltd
152 Craven Road
Newbury Berks RG14 5NR
Phone 01635-230272 and fax 01635-44804
email: publish@threshold-press.co.uk
www.threshold-press.co.uk

British Library Cataloguing in Publication Data
A catalogue record for this book is available from the British Library

ISBN 978-1-903152-20-1

Printed in England by Biddles Ltd, Kings Lynn

Acknowledgements
This project is funded by the Higher Education Funding Council for England (HEFCE)
and the Department for Employment and Learning (DEL) under the Fund for the
Development of Teaching and Learning (FDTL).

   The authors and publisher are grateful to the Higher Education Academy for permis-
sion to reproduce Yorke and Knight's 39 Aspects of employability (Appendix 1) and their
USEM model (Chapter 1, Figure 2).

Contents

Figures

Tables

Foreword

This is a most timely and apposite engagement with the issue of employability and higher education's ability to deliver. There is much pressure in the United Kingdom and many other countries for universities to play a prominent role in preparing students for the knowledge economy. In practice this means ensuring that students develop a range of employability skills to better fit them for an effective role in the economy and society. It doesn't just mean the ability to get a job.

Higher education is not the sole determinant of students' employability by any means. Individuals develop skills at university through extracurricular activities and, indeed, many have a set of employability skills and abilities that they bring with them to higher education. Furthermore, employability skills are further developed and enhanced in the workplace, aided in some cases by continuous professional development. The impact of the workplace on learning and the development of a range of skills and abilities is one reason why work experience, especially in the form of structured placements (internships) is such an important element of student employability.

Employability is not something that exists in a vacuum and what is regarded as evidence of employability varies with the economic and social context. Where skills shortages occur and graduates are in high demand, employers are more inclined to accept a more modest array of attributes and this changes when there is an oversupply of graduates.

This excellent text grasps the employability debate by the horns and explores the way employability is addressed by higher education and embedded in curricula. It draws on the hospitality, leisure, sport and tourism industries to identify demand and explore how employability has been embedded, highlighting areas such as PDP, dedicated modules and work-related learning.

The book doesn't shrink from the thorny issues of employability performance indicators, responsibility for employability, institutional strategies, curriculum developments and the tricky issue of assessment of employability. As the authors boldly state: 'Employability is here to stay and the research being conducted on how best to embed it into a university education means that practices can only improve.' A sentiment that I would heartily endorse and commend to you.

Professor Lee Harvey

I

Employability and Higher Education
Key issues

In an increasingly competitive and volatile graduate employment market students must develop greater ownership of their employability skills if they are to maximise their potential for a successful career. While the connection between higher education (HE) and the economy is well established, there is considerable evidence that HE is increasingly expected to contribute to the labour market and national wealth by equipping students with skills for employment (Little, 2004). In the UK, the Leitch review reinforced this point stating:

> there is a direct correlation between skills, productivity and employment. Unless the UK can build on reforms to schools, colleges and universities and make its skills base one of its strengths, UK business will find it increasingly difficult to compete
> (Leitch, 2006: 3).

At a European level, a key goal of the Bologna process is to 'create a European space for higher education in order to enhance the employability and mobility of citizens' (CRE, 2005: 4). With Bologna making an impact on the development of HE well beyond European boundaries and as far afield as Australia, the USA and South America, the link between education and employment would appear stronger than ever before.

The UK Government has set ambitious targets for raising skills levels of the population and they have made it clear that universities need to play a central role in up-skilling the workforce. The Department of Innovation, Universities & Skills (DIUS) Report *Higher Education at Work. High Skills: High Value* stresses the need for more people to experience higher education, not only for economic reasons, but also for the social benefits believed to derive from having a more educated population (DIUS, 2008). This in itself raises considerable challenges for HE as they expand their provision and increase the diversity of the student body (e.g. more mature students, more work based learning programmes, etc). The predicted growth in demand for graduates will serve to increase pressure on higher education institutions (HEIs) to demonstrate how they are tackling employability. This chapter reviews some of the key issues facing HEIs in relation to employability, and highlights the challenges which need to be addressed. This will set the context for later chapters which evaluate how successfully HEIs are responding to the increasing demands placed on them by key stakeholders.

The concept of employability

Employability is a concept which interacts with a range of discourses in today's higher education environment (Yorke and Knight, 2003). Defining employability is not as straightforward a task as might first appear. According to Lees (2002) employability is a multifaceted concept open to a range of interpretations and definitions. Many authors observe that a distinction must firstly be drawn between **employment** and **employability** (see for example Yorke and Knight, 2007). Employment it can be argued is synonymous with 'having a job', whereas employability is associated with 'possessing qualities that facilitate and enhance employment opportunities'. Harvey (2004: 3) defines employability in its core sense:

> as the acquisition of attributes (knowledge, skills and abilities) that make graduates more likely to be successful in their chosen occupations (whether paid employment or not).

Employability is viewed as being beyond solely getting a job, with emphasis placed on learning and ability (Harvey, 2004). A widely accepted definition of employability is derived from research conducted by the Enhancing Student Employability Coordination Team (ESECT – Yorke, 2004). Based on several years of research with key stakeholders ESECT have produced the following definition:

> a set of achievements, understandings and personal attributes that make individuals more likely to gain employment and be successful in their chosen occupations.

Figure 1 depicts the many facets of employability development and demonstrates clearly that employability is a **process** rather than a **product** of education (Harvey and Morey, 2002; Lees, 2002; LTSN, 2002). Harvey and Morey (2002)

Figure 1   *The model of graduate employability development*

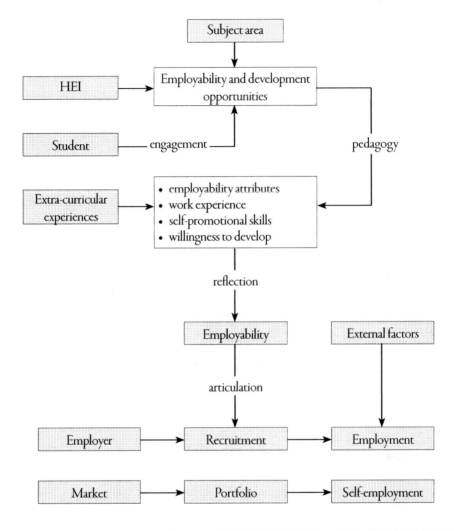

explicate further on the process of employability and state that 'employability is about how individuals engage with opportunities, and reflect and articulate their skills and experiences'. The diagram also emphasises the importance of student engagement with a wide range of opportunities and highlights the role of work experience and extra curricular activities in enabling students to develop their employability.

While Figure 1 is a useful overview of the process of employability development, clarification is needed on what 'employability attributes' are and how they may be acquired. A key model underpinning much of the current thinking in this area is commonly referred to as the 'USEM model' and is presented in Figure 2 (Yorke and Knight, 2006: 5). This model demonstrates the link between curriculum and employability, and articulates the importance of four inter-related components of:

Understanding – subject understanding is an obvious outcome of higher education and the term suggests depth of knowledge

Skills (or skilful practice) – refers to skilled practices that demonstrate awareness of and responsiveness to context, as opposed to narrowly-conceived notions of what are often termed 'key skills'

Efficacy beliefs – student's self-theories and personal qualities that influence the student's ability to see all tasks as opportunities for learning, and a belief that they can 'make a difference' – this is linked explicitly to self-confidence and self-esteem

Meta-cognition – encompasses 'learning how to learn' and student's awareness of how they learn, and also their capacity to reflect on/in/for action

The model provides an interesting view of employability and should stimulate thinking about implications for curriculum design. Yorke and Knight (2003: 6) explain the link thus:

Figure 2   *The USEM model of Yorke and Knight (2006)*

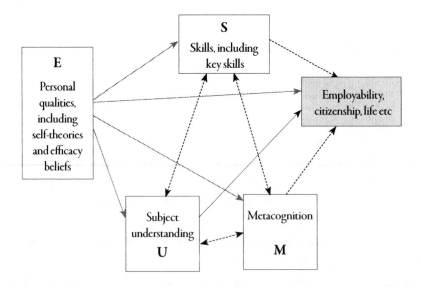

Source: Yorke, M. and Knight, P. T. (2006) Embedding employability into the curriculum. Learning and Employability Series One. York: HEA Enhancing Student Employability Co-ordination Team

Good curriculum designs will continue to be attentive to helping learners to construct understandings of the subject matter and maintain the more recent interest in developing a number of skilful practices or 'skills'. However, they will also show care for the development of positive efficacy beliefs, meta-cognition and other complex achievements that employers value.

Although the USEM model is highly regarded and underpins a large body of scholarly research on employability, it does not offer the practical solutions some educators are looking for when designing curricula to incorporate employability development.

Other models of employability have been presented which draw on the USEM concept, but claim to have much greater practical value when it comes to embedding employability into curricula. For example Dacre Pool and Sewell (2007) at the Centre for Employability (CfE) at the University of Central Lancashire have been working for more than 10 years to develop an applied model of employability. Central to the model are notions of **self-esteem, self-confidence** and **efficacy** as well as **reflection**. In addition the model incorporates five components referred to as 'CareerEDGE' (a useful mnemonic for the components):

Career Development Learning

Experience (work & life)

Degree subject knowledge, understanding & skills

Generic skills

Emotional intelligence

This model effectively demonstrates the interrelatedness of key employability components and the significance of developing the efficacy-related attributes. Dacre Pool and Sewell believe their model offers a practical approach to the planning of programmes and the embedding of employability into curricula, and the model is freely available for use by other HE practitioners. The team at CfE are also working on developing a measurement tool based on the model with which students can evaluate their employability and plan for their development.

Despite the burgeoning research on employability and availability of a wide range of models purporting to explain it, employability itself remains a contentious concept open to a 'plethora of micro-interpretations' (Harvey, 2003). This can make the task of curriculum development particularly difficult.

The growing importance of employability

According to McNair (2003), graduate employability has become a more important issue for institutions. This is:

because of the changing nature of the graduate labour market, mass participation in HE, pressures on student finance, competition to recruit students and
expectations of students, employers, parents and government (expressed in quality audit and league tables).

On a broader level, it has been noted that higher education, through the generation and dissemination of knowledge, directly impacts economic competitiveness on a national and international level (Brown et al, 2003; CIHE, 2003; UUK,
2007; DIUS, 2008).

The significance of the UK HE system to the wider economy has been generally acknowledged since the Robbins Report was published in 1963. However,
this relationship has been made more explicit in recent years and it was with the
publication of the Dearing Report (1997) that the connection found prominent
expression. Dearing strongly expressed the need for a globally competitive economy containing highly skilled, highly trained and highly motivated graduates
who could perform effectively on the world's stage. This coupled with the further
development of human-capital theory (Becker, 1975), which asserts that one role
of government is to provide and nurture conditions which will increase the pool
of skilled labour, has created a fertile forum for the discourse of 'employability' to
flourish.

The changing nature of the graduate-labour market

Dearing (1997) stated that 'learning should be increasingly responsive to employment needs and include the development of general skills, widely valued in
employment'; however, the labour market is changing dramatically and at a
much faster pace than in the past. Emerging markets and rapid expansion of the
knowledge economy means that the same set of employability skills which were
in demand ten or even five years ago may not be required in the evolving graduate-
employment market. Employers are increasingly seeking flexible recruits who can
work effectively in the 'de-layered, down-sized, information-technology driven
and innovative' organisations in existence today (Harvey et al, 1997: 1).

Employers are seeking people who can do more than just respond to change,
they need those who can lead change. McNair (2003) comments on the speed of
labour-market development and notes that a higher percentage of the workforce
is employed in small and medium enterprises (SMEs), a trend also reflected in
graduate-employment statistics. While this may offer opportunities to gain early
responsibility in less structured and hierarchical work environments, graduates
need to have the skills to create rewarding graduate roles role in what Purcell and

Elias (2004) refer to as 'niche-graduate occupations'. Niche-graduate occupations are those:

> where the majority of incumbents are not graduates, but within which there are stable or growing specialist niches that require higher education skills and knowledge (Purcell and Elias, 2003: 5).

Students therefore need to be equipped with skills which enable them to 'grow' jobs to graduate level. HE has been criticised by some as being too slow to recognise the changing nature of the labour market and is producing graduates who are ill equipped to deal with the realities of graduate employment (CBI, 2006).

Government policy to widen participation in HE, aiming to increase the proportion of 18–30 year olds to 50 per cent by 2010, will no doubt have a significant impact on the supply of graduates in the labour market. According to Elias and Purcell (2004) participation rates in UK HE almost doubled in the decade 1991–2001, from 1.2 million students to 2.1 million. Such rapid expansion has raised concerns that the increase in the number of highly qualified individuals may not be coupled with an equivalent rise in demand for their skills and qualifications (Brown and Hesketh, 2004; Brynin, 2002; Keep and Mayhew, 1996, 1999 in Elias and Purcell, 2004). While Elias and Purcell (2004) conclude that the expansion of HE at the end of the twentieth century has been primarily positive, Purcell et al (2005: 16) express concern that 'the fit between the supply of graduates and employers' demand for their knowledge and skills clearly falls some way short of ideal'.

There are mixed reports about whether demand for graduates will be affected by increasing participation in higher education. The supply of graduates has been steadily rising and there were 258,000 graduates in 1997 compared with 319,000 in 2007 (HESA, 2007). Despite rising numbers leaving HE, according to DIUS (2008), demand for graduates remains high and the latest report by the Association of Graduate Recruiters (AGR 2007) suggests that the number of graduate vacancies increased by 15.1 per cent in 2007. Both DIUS and AGR do however raise concerns about the mismatch between what employers are looking for and the skills graduates possess (see Chapter 2 for a more detailed analysis of skills). Despite much controversy about the impact of increasing student numbers, it is indisputable that graduates are facing a changing, more competitive labour market and they need to be prepared accordingly.

The changing nature of the higher education landscape

Beyond pressures facing graduates in the labour market, universities are facing increasing demands to account for what they do and prospective students and parents are becoming discerning 'customers' when shopping for the most suitable HEI (McNair, 2003). Given the importance of employability in the equation, institutions cannot overlook the significance of developing this aspect of provision. Allison et al (2002) allude to the pressures facing HEIs as evidenced by the publication of increasing numbers of performance indicators and guidance documents such as the QAA *Code of Practice for Careers Education, Information and Guidance* (2001) and the Harris *Review of Careers Services* (2001).

Yorke and Knight (2002: 4) have expressed some concern about the way in which statistics on employment rates used in league tables can distract HEIs from the important task of enhancing employability. They state that:

> once employment rates become an institutional performance indicator (HE-FCE, 2001), there is a pernicious backwash as institutions seek to 'improve their scores' since they know that these scores will end up in the so-called 'league tables' published in the press.

Consequently:

> there is a danger that maximising the score will command more institutional attention than fulfilling the educational aim of enhancing employability.

Higher Education in the UK has gone through considerable change during the last two decades. The move from an elitist system to one of mass participation has been highly significant. Shelley (2005) indicates that the number of 18–30 year olds in HE rose from 12 per cent in the 1980s to 43 per cent by 2002. This he points out has not been matched with commensurate levels of funding and between 1977 and 1997 government expenditure per student fell by 40 per cent. In recent years however funding levels have improved with HEFCE announcing a figure of £6,706 million in recurrent funding for 2006–07 to universities and colleges in England (HEFCE, 2006).

Increased funding levels have led to systems of accountability being put in place. These in turn have led to the development of managerial practices intended to promote new efficiency and customer-focused, customer-led policy frameworks which should ensure success in a new competitive market. In the eyes of commentators such as Bekhradnia (2005) the last decade has seen a mixture of successes and failures of managerial initiatives.

For some commentators (e.g. Brown and Lauder, 1999; Green, 1993) these policy directives coupled with the emphasis placed on the contribution of HE to the global economy has led to the 'marketisation' and the 'commodification' of HE and its teaching. Brown and Lauder (1999) contend that there has been a movement towards a 'neo-Fordist' approach to HE in which teaching and learning is now emulating the Fordist manufacturing processes of the early twentieth century. This concept was characterised by the production assembly line 'just-in-time' unitisation production methods of manufacturing industries. For HE this manifests itself in several ways which Brown and Lauder describe as: learner organisations with emphasis on 'numerical' flexibility (i.e. outcome-related education and cost-driven agendas), mass production of standardised products (i.e. modularisation/unitisation of curricula), and emphasis on quality systems to ensure standardisation which result in a bland mechanistic experience of learning.

The changing expectations of HE stakeholders

As mentioned in the previous section, students are increasingly seen as customers in HE. Ramsden (2007: 4) writes:

> students are not customers in any conventional sense of the word. The product or service they acquire derives value from their striving to achieve it and their achievement of it is determined to a significant extent by those who supply it. Most students want to be treated as collaborators in a process of developing understanding.

Although not necessarily a contested view, evidence suggests that parents and students are increasingly aware of the financial relationship they enter into with an institution when embarking on a programme of study (Baker, 2008). Students expect that the investment in their education will reap benefits in their future employment and they are much more likely to expect the HEI to take a lead in providing opportunities which speed their progress into the graduate labour market. While there is evidence that graduates continue to enjoy high wage premiums over non-graduates (graduates earn around 20–25 per cent more than similar non-graduates – HESA, 2007), increases in tuition and living costs means that graduates' salary expectations are ever higher. The expectation is that HEIs should not only provide an excellent grounding in the subject studied but also that they will provide excellent information and resources to enhance employability, thus increasing pressure on universities in relation to resourcing such initiatives and finding space in the curriculum to deliver them.

Employers' expectations of the role of HEIs in delivering 'employable' graduates seems also to be changing, and they are quick to criticise when they feel students do not have the right skills. Atkins (1999) argues that employers often expect graduates to make a positive contribution to the company from 'day one'.

Companies, especially small firms, also claim they cannot afford (and should not be expected to) bear the costs associated with training new recruits in generic employment skills. By implication therefore, it is the responsibility of HEIs to provide students with the necessary employment skills to ensure that they are 'oven-ready' (i.e. able to 'hit the ground running') and preferably 'self-basting' (i.e. self-sufficient in managing their careers) (Atkins, 1999; Maher, 2004).

The Association of Graduate Recruiters (AGR) report from 2005 states that more than 50 per cent of the employers surveyed thought many graduates lacked important employability skills, and findings from their latest *Graduate Recruitment Survey* (Winter 2007) highlighted the following inadequacies:

o   lack of applicants with the right combination of skills (e.g. team-working and leadership)
o   lack of applicants with the right qualifications for specific job roles
o   issues with specific geographical locations
o   applicants' perceptions of the industry sector.

Elias and Purcell (2004: 61) also cite AGR (2002) and Mason (1999, 2002) in identifying that many employers who require certain graduate skills (particularly with reference to numeracy-based subjects) have continued to report skills shortages. There continues then to be discontent among some employers that university programmes are not producing graduates with appropriate skills and Medhat (2003), in an article for the *Times Higher Educational Supplement*, goes so far as to state that 'there is a chasm between what industry wants and what universities provide', although he does not spell out the exact nature of this 'chasm'.

From a political standpoint, the view of recent government ministers has been clear. In response to findings about skills mismatches and the skill needs of employers announced by the AGR, Bill Rammell, then Higher Education Minister, responded saying:

> that is why we have placed much emphasis on the growth of foundation degrees, because they are vocational higher education qualifications designed with employers.

In a subsequent address, Rammell, an advocate of vocational education and in particular foundation degrees, stated that after successfully completing a foundation degree 'you'll get a good job at the end of it' (www.gradjobs.co.uk). While this may be so, such a statement perhaps reinforces a rather one-dimensional view of the concept of employability.

In 2005 Rammell urged universities to play a greater role in vocational education stressing:

we all ought to be thinking more seriously about why only £130 million of the £4 billion employer market in continuing-professional development for their staff was being spent on university-accredited provision   (Curtis, 2005).

While Rammell may be correct in urging institutions to bid competitively for training contracts, this view contrasts strongly from the findings of Harvey et al (1997) which conclude 'employers expect a degree to provide a profound, broad education rather than attempt to train someone for a specific job'.

Keep (2003) observes 'the history of vocational education and training policy is a saga of failure littered with discarded institutions and schemes'. In response to government's new skills strategy, Keep asserts skills shortages are not to blame for a lack of UK economic performance and that a move towards a knowledge-driven economy is a process which could span almost two decades. Bynner (1998: 5) states:

> vocational education and training in the broader sense needs to pursue goals that transcend the narrow aim of equipping young people for any kind of job instead it 'must include a commitment to improving education and employment prospects on a lifelong basis'.

The publication of the Harris Report (2001) and the *QAA Code of Practice on Career Education, Information and Guidance* (QAA, 2001) have added further impetus to the debate on graduate employability and while HEIs themselves have always placed importance on the employability of their graduates and many provide support for career-skills development, there is now a level of expectation on universities not previously seen.

Conclusion

While there appears to be some consensus amongst key stakeholders on the importance of addressing employability, there remains a debate on how best this can be achieved and, indeed, the extent to which HE can influence this aspect of student development. Brown et al (2003) propose that employability varies according to economic conditions, outlining the duality of the concept in terms of absolute and relative dimensions. The absolute dimension is associated with the skills and attributes possessed by an individual while the relative dimension relies on the supply of jobs in the labour market. While higher education seemingly has a responsibility to develop the absolute dimension in each individual student, the impact of the relative dimension on resultant student employability cannot be overlooked.

Government policy insists that employability be addressed, while increasing competition in the labour and education markets necessitates its inclusion on institutional agendas for learning and teaching. A key challenge facing students and educationalists alike is managing the transition from higher education to work (Knight and Yorke, 2004: 11). There is a need to develop curriculum interventions which enable students to make clear connections between their education and work, and help them recognise the relevance/value of their studies. Harvey et al (1997: 1) observe that organisations want people to 'help them transform their organisations' and to 'use higher level-skills, such as analysis, critique, synthesis, and multi-layered communication to facilitate innovative teamwork'. Higher-education curricula (and assessment tasks in particular) must therefore aim to foster the development of these abilities.

2

The Great Skills Debate

As we saw in the previous chapter, employability in HE is by no means a recent area for debate and explicit references to the labour market can be found in the Robbins Report published in 1963. However, almost 50 years after Robbins, employability is a subject which continues to cause much controversy in academia. Some commentators feel the debate has highlighted a fundamental discrepancy between the academics' and the government's views of what education is for (Lees 2002). Lomas (1997), citing Tapper and Salter (1995), discusses the ideological struggle between those who view HEIs as having a primarily economic purpose (arguably the government and employers) and those who are driven to protect the 'traditional liberal ideal' of education (the academics).

The concept of liberal education and associated prestige is deeply rooted in the nineteenth and twentieth centuries (Sanderson, 1993). Many academics feel that the employability agenda is too driven by government and employers and this represents an attack on academic freedom. Hirst (1965), one of the main advocates of liberal education, expresses the point succinctly and states that; liberal education is:

> based on the nature of knowledge itself, and not on the ... demands of society, or the whims of politicians. Liberal education is concerned with developing the mind and helping students to understand their culture'.

> (cited in Lomas, 1997: 111)

While many consider this a rather romantic view of HE, the ideological arguments which see education as a means of developing knowledge and the mind lie at the heart of much of the controversy surrounding the employability debate. The use of the term 'skills' in the HE arena has caused particular unrest and, for some academics, presents the clearest indication that universities are being required to train students for employment rather than educate them. Even those who can appreciate the value of developing students' employability can become defensive and critical of the 'skills' terminology and feel uncomfortable with the expectation that they should teach employability skills and attributes in the classroom (Lees, 2002). Rather, many academics feel that the curriculum should focus on developing the students understanding of the subject, with softer employability 'skills' (e.g. communication, team working, problem solving, etc) emerging as a natural by-product of the students' educational experiences and mostly the responsibility of the student themselves – or the university careers office.

Advocates of employability, however, strongly believe that scepticism surrounding the vocabulary is an unfortunate distraction which has led academics to neglect a critical area of student development. Harvey (2000b) sees employability as supportive of good learning, rather than in opposition to it, and points out that academics are being asked to consider *how* they teach their subject – not *what* they teach. Curricula can be designed to both enhance employability *and* develop the self more generally, and the two should not be viewed as mutually exclusive. Despite the disagreements which exist, there are increasingly signs that universities are addressing the issue of enhancing employability and acknowledge that they have some responsibility to help students develop skills which will be important for their employment. In order to develop students' employability it is necessary first to have some insight into what makes graduates successful at work and how those skills or attributes can be developed at university.

This chapter evaluates the research evidence to establish what skills and attributes are thought to be important for success in the labour market. The first section examines the way in which 'skills' terminology has evolved in HE in order to set the context for later discussions about graduate attributes. The next section provides an overview of some of the research on graduate skills and seeks to determine which particular skills are highly valued by employers. This section will also examine whether these are the same skills valued by students/graduates and educators. The next section explores whether gaps exist in graduate skills and the final part of the chapter summarises implications for enhancing employability in HE.

What do we mean by employability skills?

Discourse about skills and competencies can be traced back through several decades. Payne (2000) observes that, for more than two decades, policy makers in Britain have repeatedly emphasised the relationship between national economic competitiveness and skill levels. Payne (2000) charts the evolution of the term skill back to the 1950s and 60s when it equated to hard technical ability and 40 years ago the Carr Report spoke of 'skilled craftsmen'. The concept of 'skill' has broadened in recent years moving away from earlier manual-based associations (Ainley, 1993; Keep and Mayhew, 1999 in Payne, 2000). Today's discourse regularly employs terms such as 'employability skills', 'key skills' and 'management skills' and the concept of 'skill' has

> expanded almost exponentially to include a veritable galaxy of 'soft', 'generic', 'transferable', 'social' and 'interactional' skills, frequently indistinguishable from personal characteristics, behaviours and attitudes
>
> (Payne 2000: 54, citing Keep & Mahew 1999).

As with the development of the skills concept, the notion of graduate competencies and attributes can also be charted through the decades. Innumerable studies have produced lists of the graduate attributes desired by employers which vary in their degrees of complexity (Harvey et al, 1997). Many of the studies have resulted in the generation of useful indicators of the attributes and skills required by graduates as they enter the labour market and Harvey et al (1997) affirm that the lists show strong similarities across academic disciplines, employment sectors and international borders. It would seem to be the case that despite some very minor changes (such as increase in demand for skills including flexibility, interpersonal skills and team-working) there has been 'very little change in the last 20-30 years in the sorts of attributes [employers] want' (Harvey et al, 1997). The reported gaps in the skills graduates possess and those valued by employers appear to have changed very little either and this has led Harvey et al (1997: 64) to ask 'Is anybody listening?' – presumably meaning anyone in HE. These issues are examined in more detail in the following section.

Graduate skills: what do employers want?

Many studies exist which have resulted in the production of lists of graduate attributes desired by employers. Some of these studies are sophisticated, attempting to prioritise these attributes in terms of their importance to employers. Others go further still and explore how satisfied employers are with the attributes of graduates (Harvey et al, 1992 cited in Harvey, Moon and Geall, 1997: 64). Little

(2003: 7) notes:

> within the UK, particular attention has been focused on a specific set of 'key skills' in higher education – generally described as: oral and written communication skills; numerical abilities; computer skills; ability to work in a team; problem-solving; learning abilities/reflective thinking, assessing one's own work'.

Similarly Prospects (2003) report that 'employers often desire a consistent set of core skills, independent of degree subject'. These include both interactive and personal attributes. **Interactive attributes** include communication skills, interpersonal skills and team working skills and **personal attributes** include intellect and problem-solving, analytic, critical and reflective ability, willingness to learn, flexibility, adaptability and risk-taking. These qualities/abilities must be coupled with a grasp of the world of work and a honed sense of commercial awareness (Prospects, 2003).

Appendix 3 is a summary table of the skills listed in five key research studies and one can see clearly that there is a great deal of similarity between the graduate skills which employers value. Examining the lists more closely it is clear that many employers view social skills and personality attributes as more important than degree subject (although this will obviously vary between employers and depend on the nature of the job). An examination of the lists in Table 1 demonstrates that the following skills are most often cited:

Communication skills

Both written and oral skills are cited in all the studies and often include the ability to influence others and present ideas persuasively, in addition to literacy.

Team work/working with others

Another skill which appears in all lists and not only involves ability to work effectively in a team, but also ability to network and build relationships and to cooperate with others.

Self-confidence

Again mentioned in all lists and incorporates self-belief and ability to promote oneself in a positive way (closely related to the concept of self-efficacy in the USEM model).

Self-motivation

A key attribute which may also include willingness/motivation to learn, 'proactivity', drive/energy and enthusiasm.

Self-management

Includes the ability to manage time and tasks, to plan and prioritise and to be independent. Related skills might be considered to **ability to work under pressure** and **ability to cope with uncertainty** as these both require a high degree of planning and organisational ability.

Problem-solving

Is cited in almost all studies as a key skill and involves being able to identify key issues and the ability to develop practical solutions.

Numeracy

All studies mention numeracy as a key skill and one which involves the ability to manipulate and understand numerical information/data.

Commitment

Employers value employees who are dedicated and trustworthy and who demonstrate high levels of integrity. This skill may also incorporate reliability and dependability.

Intellectual skills

In the Reuters study this includes the ability to assimilate or abstract information, evaluate evidence and synthesise arguments – in other studies this is referred to as analytic ability or intellectual ability.

Other skills

A range of other skills cited as important include **flexibility/adaptability; IT/computer literacy; ability to work under pressure;** and **ability to cope with uncertainty**.

This list of graduate skills appears in one form or another in many government publications and is summarised in the 2008 DIUS consultation document *Higher Education at Work. High Skills: High Value*: The report is worth quoting at length:

> Employers particularly value broad 'employability' skills. This is one of the strongest messages from employers to government and is backed up by recent research suggesting employers tend to look for graduates who exhibit skills and attributes such as communication, motivation, independence, analysis, confidence and problem-solving. These cognitive skills are best learned young. HE providers, therefore, have a crucial contribution to make and should ensure they are developing and expanding students' existing cognitive skills.
>
> (DIUS, 2008: 14)

The above quotation is interesting as it stresses that employability skills are about **cognitive development** and this may be seen as an attempt by government to appease (or draw in) those academics who feel that employability development is separate from a student's broader intellectual development. Employability advocates have long argued that the two are closely linked and often stress the importance of not focusing too much on 'key skills' at the expense of developing the self more generally (see Harvey et al, 1997 & 2003; Little, 2001; Yorke & Knight, 2003). Lees (2002) in her review of the employability literature for the Higher Education Academy stresses the emphasis on the development of the intellect in enabling students to become critical thinkers and innovators – skills which employers value highly.

Harvey et al (1997) emphasise that employers are seeking recruits who are intelligent, flexible, innovative and adaptable as well as skilled inter-personally. Essentially organisations are seeking staff who 'can do more than respond to change', staff 'who can anticipate and lead change'. In addition to this:

> employers are looking for adaptive people who fit in, they also want them to be intelligent, rounded people who have a depth of understanding, can apply themselves, take responsibility and develop their role in the organisation – to be educated rather than trained (Harvey et al, 1997).

Clearly, there exists a body of research and literature that attempts to define and encapsulate which skills are required by employers and to translate this into clearly articulated and defined capability statements. Harvey's (1997) research suggests that employers in the UK value generic skills more highly than discipline-based specific skills. In quoting one employer Harvey provides an example of this:

> I don't care what you did your degree in, I really don't … Even in areas like finance, I don't necessarily want a finance-trained human being. It is as much if not more about personal traits, personal drive and ambition. You could be managing director of this company with a degree in sociology.

> (Director, commercial operations, vehicle manufacturer in Harvey et al, 1997)

Although it is clear that the softer/more generic skills are very important in employers eyes one must be careful not to dismiss subject knowledge altogether. Subject expertise may be less emphasised by some employers as it is taken for granted that the attainment of the degree confers this knowledge – and is therefore a given. For others the training of the mind and empowerment of the worker comes through the learning of a discipline and, although the specific subject of the degree may be less important; that the student has studied for and attained a degree is indicative of a certain level of intellectual attainment.

It is interesting to note that research conducted with graduates, students and educators on employability reveals similar sets of skills as those found in employer studies. Elias and Purcell (2004), Harvey et al (1997) and Little (2001), among others, have conducted extensive research with graduates and students on their perceptions of employability skills. Important skills cited are: spoken and written communication, problem-solving skills, team-working skills, IT and numeracy skills, and management skills.

Possibly the most comprehensive list of graduate attributes has been complied by Yorke and Knight (2006) and derived from many years research conducted under the remit of the Skills *Plus* project and ESECT. The 39 attributes list located in Appendix 1 categorises skills into three broad areas:

Personal qualities
which include self-awareness, self-confidence, willingness to learn, emotional intelligence, independence and adaptability

Core skills
including self-management, written and oral communication, critical analysis and numeracy

Process skills
including problem-solving, team working, computer literacy, coping with ambiguity/uncertainty, acting morally (i.e. integrity), planning and prioritising.

The 39-attributes list is wide-ranging and presents many attributes not always explicitly mentioned in employer-derived lists. Ethical sensitivity, reflectiveness, global awareness, and resolving conflict are skills not often cited in employer surveys. Ability to work cross-culturally and language skills tend only to be mentioned rarely and only in those studies which deliberately target large international employers in their surveys (see Archer and Davison's report for CIHE 2008, for example). Commercial awareness is also an attribute from the list which is conspicuously absent from many of the employer lists, even though 'a lack of business awareness' amongst graduates was cited as a key area of concern for employers in two of the most recent surveys (AGR, 2007; CBI, 2008). The subject benchmark statements produced for QAA by groups of academics to help universities develop their courses also use very similar terminology to the 39 attributes for transferable and disciplinary/professional skills. So there is clearly a commonality of views among the different stakeholders regarding skills.

Graduate skills: where are the gaps?
Skills gaps exist where employers consider that employees are not fully proficient at their job. The National Employer Skills Survey (NESS) provides a good barometer for measuring employers' perceptions of workforce skills and is one of

the most comprehensive surveys of its kind. NESS is produced by the Learning and Skills Council (LSC) in collaboration with the Department for Innovation, Universities and Skills (DIUS) and the Sector Skills Development Agency (SSDA). Conducted each year since 2003, the latest (2007) survey includes data from more than 79,000 employer interviews. The NESS website states:

> With increasing international competition, it is more important than ever to understand the skills issues facing employers. Only then can we work with companies to help them address their skills and recruitment needs, thereby enabling the British economy to remain competitive in the global market. The National Employer Skills Survey (NESS) gathers and analyses data on the issues employers face in terms of recruitment, skills gaps and training   (NESS, 2007).

Despite improvements in the perception of the work-readiness of young people recruited direct from education, significant minorities of employers feel that recruits from school, college or university are poorly or very poorly prepared for work. One in eight (12 per cent) of those recruiting young people direct from higher education feel they have been poorly or very poorly prepared for work (this compares with 27 per cent of 16-year-old school leavers, and 21 per cent of 17- or 18-year-old school leavers). Where the recruits are poorly prepared for the jobs they are recruited to, this is most commonly in terms of **personal attributes** and/or because of their **lack of experience**, rather than explicitly in terms of skills. The data suggest that the longer an individual spends in education the more likely they are to be equipped with the personal attributes which employers require, although this is perhaps as likely to be a function of age as of the benefits of education per se (NESS, 2007).

In terms of specific skills, NESS results reveal that skills which staff lack tend to be in the soft-skill areas, particularly **communication, customer handling, team working** and **problem-solving skills**. These skills were lacking in two-fifths to a half of all cases of skills gaps. **Technical** and **practical skills** are lacking among over two-in-five employees who have skills gaps (45 per cent). Much less common, though still found in around a quarter of cases where staff lacked proficiency, was insufficient general **information-technology user skills** and a lack of **management skills**. Clearly gaps in regard to managerial skills have particular potential to impact on business performance and growth. Results suggest that three per cent of managers have gaps in their management skills (NESS, 2003).

In NESS 2007:

> the skills that employers reported (on a spontaneous basis) to be lacking among young people recruited direct from education who were poorly prepared for

Table 1 Skills lacking among young recruits direct from education (spontaneous)

Column percentages (%)	16-year-old school leavers		17- or 18-yr-old school or college leavers		University or HE leavers	
	2005	2007	2005	2007	2005	2007
Unweighted base	2,173	2,107	2,581	2,618	1,020	1,096
Weighted base	31,138	28,600	36,460	37,022	15,656	15,824
Lack of life/working-world experience	16	16	14	12	12	18
Oral communication skills	16	15	13	14	9	12
Lack of motivation/enthusiasm/commitment	13	14	14	16	11	9
Poor education/general knowledge/skills	12	13	13	10	7	9
Work ethic/poor attitude to work	11	11	8	11	2	11
Time keeping skills/punctuality	10	10	9	12	6	7
Literacy skills	10	9	8	7	6	8
Social/people skills	10	9	6	8	3	7
Technical, practical or job-specific skills	10	8	12	11	18	20
Numeracy skills	8	8	8	7	6	4
Experience (business/practical)	8	7	6	7	6	12
Poor attitude (inc. manners/respect)	7	7	7	6	4	2
Common sense	7	7	7	8	3	6
Customer-service skills	4	7	4	7	3	8
Not prepared to work long hours	4	5	6	5	12	4
Initiative	4	4	2	3	1	2
Confidence	4	3	4	3	7	2
Written-communication skills	3	2	2	3	5	3
Discipline	2	2	2	3	1	2
Responsibility	2	2	3	2	1	1
Personal appearance/presentation	2	2	2	2	*	1
Team-working skills	2	1	2	1	1	1
Basic IT/computer skills	1	1	1	1	2	3
Interview skills	1	1	1	1	1	1
Office/administration skills	1	1	2	1	2	2
Organisational skills	1	1	1	1	1	2
Other	4	8	6	6	9	7
Don't know	1	*	1	2	1	*
Any mention of lack of motivation/commitment or work ethic/poor attitude to work or poor attitude (manners/respect) or not prepared to work long hours	35	32	35	33	28	23

Base: All employers that have recruited each type of 16- to 24-yr-old leaver from education in previous 12 months and who say some of these recruits were poorly prepared.

work are shown in Table 1. When comparing the list of skills and attributes lacking across the three educational output groups, it should be borne in mind that employers' expectations of these three groups will vary considerably. For that reason the analysis focuses on changes from 2005 within each group, rather than the differences across groups.

Although employers are generally satisfied with the skills of those leaving HE, there were still a significant number who mentioned skills that were more commonly reported as lacking in young recruits from higher education. Twenty per cent cited **technical, practical** or **job-specific skills,** whilst just under a fifth (18 per cent) perceived their poorly prepared graduate recruits to **lack experience of the working world** – significantly higher than in 2005 (12 per cent). Perhaps this is related to the trend for universities to make work experience optional as opposed to compulsory and certainly should give some pause for reflection for HE (Little and Harvey, 2006). A relatively large proportion, 23 per cent, mention **poor motivation, commitment and/or attitude,** including an **unwillingness to work long hours. A lack of oral communication skills** remains one of the most commonly cited problems across all three groups, and was mentioned by 12–15 per cent of employers reporting that recruits in each group had been poorly prepared for work.

NESS have provided an interesting further analysis of the skills and attributes listed as lacking (see Table 2). Figure 3 presents a breakdown of those respondents who reported skills gaps in their recruits. They have reduced the full list of skills and attributes detailed in Table 1 into three categories: **skills and competencies, personal attributes** and issues relating to **experience or length of time in work** (see Table 2 for details).

Table 2 'Net categories': ways in which recruits are poorly prepared for work

Skills and competencies	Numeracy skills; literacy skills; technical, practical or job-specific skills; basic IT/computer skills; customer-service skills; office/ administration skills; written communication skills; oral communication skills; organisational skills; team-working skills
Personal attributes	Lack of motivation/enthusiasm/commitment; work ethic/poor attitude to work; time-keeping skills/punctuality; poor attitude (inc. manners/respect); not prepared to work long hours; discipline; social/people skills; common sense; initiative; confidence; responsibility; personal appearance/presentation
Experience/maturity	Poor education/general knowledge/skills; lack of life/working world experience; lack of experience (business/practical)

*Figure 3   Ways in which young recruits are poorly prepared for work
(using NESS codes from Table 2)*

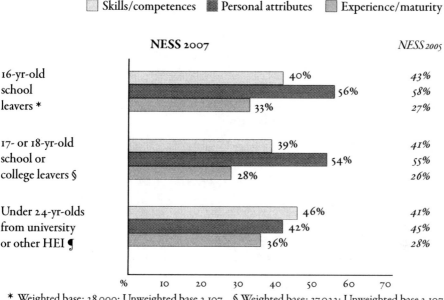

☐ Skills/competences   ■ Personal attributes   ▨ Experience/maturity

	NESS 2007	*NESS 2005*
16-yr-old school leavers *	40% / 56% / 33%	*43% / 58% / 27%*
17- or 18-yr-old school or college leavers §	39% / 54% / 28%	*41% / 55% / 26%*
Under 24-yr-olds from university or other HEI ¶	46% / 42% / 36%	*41% / 45% / 28%*

* Weighted base: 28,000; Unweighted base 2,107   § Weighted base: 37,022; Unweighted base 2,107
¶ Weighted base: 15,824; Unweighted base 1,000

Base: All employers recruiting each type of young first-jobber who they perceive to be poorly prepared
for work.

Source: Learning and Skills Council

For poorly prepared HE leavers, employers mentioned a lack of skills and competencies (46 per cent) most commonly, followed by personal attributes (42 per
cent).

Is there a skills gap?

It is important not to take such evidence at face value however. According to
Keep (2002), current concern over poor skills and correlation with economic
performance has tended to place blame on a poor supply of skills, whether this
has resulted from a lack of training or education. This approach has been criticised however by commentators who emphasise the need to explore how skills
are actually being deployed in the workplace and who identify a potential weak-
ness in demand for high-level skills (Finegold and Soskice, 1988; Ashton and
Green, 1996; Keep and Mayhew, 1999; Brown, 2001; Brown and Lauder, 2001 in
Keep, 2002). Dunne et al (2000) point out that there may be a lack of common

language of skills between HEIs and employers and there is not necessarily agreement over whether there actually is a 'skills gap' at all and, if it does exist, how big it is (Lees, 2002). Atkins (1999) notes that skills required may vary with region, size of business and type of business-market orientation. So the picture on skills is complicated and language surrounding skills even more so. This creates obvious difficulties for HEIs attempting to enhance employability and embed approaches in the curriculum.

Graduate skills: curriculum issues

Given the apparent consensus among the key stakeholders about which skills are important and on the need to address employability in HE, it seems strange that there is so little commonality in approaches taken by universities to enhance employability. There remains considerable debate on how best enhancement of employability can be achieved, and indeed the extent to which HE can influence this aspect of student development. In an extensive review of HE provision, Little (2004: 4) concludes that while there is:

> international concern that higher education should enhance graduate employability, there is little evidence of systematic thinking about how best to do it, let alone any model that can be badged as 'best practice' and adopted wholesale.

Developing a common understanding of how to enhance employability is a highly complex issue, although Knight (2001) believes government and others persist in treating it in much the same way as 'innovation', as 'something simple, to be planned, delivered and evaluated' (Knight, 2001 cited in Lees, 2002: 1).

Attempting to form a coordinated and holistic approach to skill development, government has introduced many programmes and initiatives to promote skill development and these seem to have had some impact. The DfEE Higher Education Projects Fund 1998–2000, for example, included projects to develop key and transferable skills and Harvey, Locke and Morey (2002) have reviewed the trends in institutions' approaches to embedding employability. They note that there has been a shift in HE from developing the specific employability skills within specialist modules to a more holistic approach where institutions are embedding employability and skills throughout the curriculum. They present examples of employability initiatives from different HEIs which were highly varied and based on differing philosophies.

Perhaps it is inevitable that institutions and even individual departments and academics will vary widely in their approaches to developing employability as they will be operating in the context of their own frame of reference about education, and will be dealing with students who will vary hugely in their ability and ambitions. However, it is clear from the research on employability skills that the attributes which employers value and educators recognise as important are very similar, and there is hope that such consensus in thinking can contribute to a more coherent approach to curriculum development. This is an issue to be explored further in Chapters 4 and 5.

3

The Hospitality, Leisure, Sport and Tourism Graduate Labour Market
A review of demand and supply

This chapter surveys the key data on demand for, and supply of, graduate labour in hospitality, leisure, sport and tourism (HLST). These particular sectors were the focus of a three-year research project undertaken by the authors and funded by the Higher Education Funding Council for England. HLST represents the fastest growing sector of the economy and is a major employer in the UK and worldwide. Demand for graduate labour in HLST is growing at an ever increasing rate and HE has a major role to play in supplying employers needs for highly skilled graduate recruits. (QAA, 2008)

In the context of hospitality, leisure, sport and tourism, employability has particular relevance because of the diversity of industries and the volatility of employment in the sectors, which means students face particular challenges in gaining graduate jobs. In hospitality, for example, as in many other industries, increasing levels of complexity and competition have a direct impact on the skills needed by managers working in the industry and Raybould and Wilkins (2005: 214) conclude:

> universities must change their focus from producing graduates to fill existing jobs to producing graduates who can create new jobs in a dynamic growth sector of the economy.

Maher (2005) notes that the vast majority of HLST businesses are small and may not therefore be set up to accommodate graduates, or experienced enough to exploit the skills they can bring to an organisation. Graduates therefore need to have a clear sense of ownership of employability skills which enable them to create a rewarding graduate role in what Purcell and Elias refer to as 'niche-graduate occupations' (see Chapter 1, page 7). Occupations such as entertainment/sports managers and hotel/accommodation managers are included in the 'niche' category; positions which HLST graduates frequently aspire to.

Recent reassessment of HESA First Destination Statistics on 'graduate' employment suggests that fewer HLST students than previously thought (64.7 per cent as opposed to 94.2 per cent) are entering graduate-level employment (Kingston, 2003) and many therefore may not being given the opportunity to utilise their skills. This can be a cause of dissatisfaction and may result in graduates being lost to the industry as they seek job fulfilment elsewhere. Also important to note is that employment within HLST is particularly sensitive to fluctuations in the economic cycle and students need to see the value of their abilities so that they can move freely between organisations as the economy changes. A HEFCE research report (01/30) published in 2001 provides clear evidence that demand for graduates from hospitality and related courses is very strong, and recommends 'that students are encouraged to develop realistic expectations of and recognise the opportunities for employment in the industry' (2001: 7). As reported in the newly revised *2008 Subject Benchmark Statements for HLST*, an emphasis on employability has underpinned curriculum developments in these subject areas for some time.

The HLST Labour Market: supply of graduates

The HECSU AGR *Winter Review* predicts growth in graduate vacancies across all economic sectors of 16.4 per cent for 2008. This constitutes the fifth consecutive year of growth in demand with 2008 set to enjoy the highest percentage increase in a decade (AGR, 2008). Although these figures are reported across all industries, these predictions represent an equally positive level of demand for those graduating from courses in HLST. In terms of a 'supply' of HLST graduates, educational provision in the subjects has expanded significantly over the last few years (Litteljohn and Watson, 1997).

According to figures compiled by the Association for Tourism in Higher Education, 122 institutions offered higher education courses in tourism in 2007. Findings reported by Jameson and Walmesley in 2006 indicate the number of institutions offering hospitality management courses in that year totalled 71. CHME research (2005) highlights there is clear evidence that the number of institutions offering hospitality-management courses is burgeoning.

The provision of sport and exercise-science education is also reported to be going from strength to strength. According to a search of the UCAS website there are 149 further and higher education institutions offering courses in sport and sport related areas for 2009 (UCAS, 2008). Thirty-four institutions submitted research to the sport related area in the 2001 Research Assessment Exercise with five institutions receiving a top five-star rating (HE Courses-Careers, 2008).

Each subject in the HLST grouping has its own unique set of knowledge, intellectual and subject specific skills outlined in the 2008 QAA *Benchmark Statements* and in turn reflected in the CIHE *Student Employability Profiles* (2006). The 'generic' learning outcomes for programmes across the HLST subject grouping report that graduates 'will have developed a range of skills and aptitudes, including being able to':

o Research and assess paradigms, theories, principles, concepts and factual information, and apply such skills in explaining and solving problems.
o Critically assess and evaluate evidence in the context of research methodologies and data sources.
o Critically interpret data of different kinds and appraise the strengths and weaknesses of approaches adopted.
o Describe, synthesise, interpret, analyse and evaluate information and data relevant to a professional or vocational context.
o Plan, design, execute and communicate a sustained piece of independent intellectual work which provides evidence of critical engagement with, and interpretation of, appropriate data.
o Apply knowledge to the solution of familiar and unfamiliar problems.
o Develop a sustained reasoned argument, perhaps challenging previously held assumptions.
o Demonstrate effective communication and presentation skills.
o Work effectively independently and with others.
o Take and demonstrate responsibility for their own learning and continuing personal and professional development.
o Self-appraise and reflect on practice.
o Plan, design, manage and execute practical activities using appropriate techniques and procedures whilst demonstrating high levels of relevant skills.
o Recognise and respond to moral, ethical, sustainability and safety issues which directly pertain to the context of study including relevant legislation and professional codes of conduct.
o Undertake fieldwork with continuous regard for safety and risk assessment.

Table 3 Transferable skills reported by subject in the CIHE Student Employability Profiles (2006)

Subject area	Transferable skills
Hospitality	Exercise communication and presentation skills
	Make a sustained argument with clear structure and presentation
	Interact effectively with individuals and groups, organise a team effectively and treat others' values, beliefs and opinions with respect
	Evaluate and reflect on the effectiveness of team and one's performance or contribution, including leadership of a group
	Demonstrate learning from work experience, including in some cases individual placement
	Organise work and learn independently, plan and be responsive to change
	Make independent judgements and analyse own performance in relation to personal and career development
	Apply numerical tools and techniques for handling figures and statistics using numeracy and IT skills
	Take responsibility for own learning and continuing professional development by developing the knowledge and understanding of how to learn, recognising the importance of personal development planning, the ability to demonstrate skills developed, and to present evidence
	Be reflective and self-critical and perceive self in relation to others
	Plan, design, execute and communicate a piece of independent work using appropriate media.
Leisure	Undertake fieldwork with regard to safety and risk assessment (to subject specific category)
	Exercise communication and presentation skills, numeracy and IT skills
	Work in teams and contribute effectively to group work
	Plan and manage own learning
	Apply motivation and aptitude for intellectual enquiry, critical assessment, creative innovation and a commitment to lifelong learning
	Work both independently and collaboratively
	Apply customer service and customer-satisfaction concepts to subject studied.

The transferable skills outlined in Table 3 demonstrate that HE courses in HLST are aiming to produce highly employable graduates who are responsive to the needs of the sector. The skills also correlate with those outlined in Chapter 2, and therefore confirm that skills sets are similar across course boundaries. These findings nevertheless need to be examined in the context of the current skills climate in the relevant industries and in light of the potential growth opportunities.

Table 3 Transferable skills reported by subject continued

Subject area	Transferable skills
Sport	Demonstrate competence in interactive and group skills
	Work with an ethos of teamwork and independence
	Know how to learn, adapt to changing circumstances, self-appraise and reflect on practice
	Plan and manage own development and learning
	Apply techniques of safety and risk assessment
	Exercise communication and presentation skills, numeracy and ICT skills
	Apply motivation and aptitude for intellectual enquiry, critical assessment, creative innovation and a commitment to lifelong learning
	Work both independently and collaboratively
	Apply customer service and customer satisfaction concepts and best practice to subject studied
	Demonstrate appropriate and effective coaching skills where studied
	Demonstrate learning from work experience.
Tourism	Profile on tourism graduates' transferable skills not available at time of publication.

It is estimated that by 2012 the hospitality, leisure and tourism sector will experience a sea change in terms of the demographics of its labour force, with a decrease of 19,000 in the number of low-skilled and technical workers and an increase of 41,000 managers (Labour Force Survey, 2004–05). This has implications for curriculum development within the FE and HE sectors and the types of roles graduates will be recruited into.

Employment within HLST

In the context of hospitality, leisure, travel and tourism, this sector experiences a number of challenges including: hard-to-fill vacancies (40 per cent, generally higher than the economy as a whole); high levels of labour turnover; and, a lack of technically skilled workers such as chefs (People 1st, 2006). It is predicted that by 2014 there will be a requirement of 1,642,000 workers needed in the sector (*Working Futures II*), though according to the sector skills council this is likely to be an underestimate of the ever increasing demand.

It is estimated that over a third of workers in the hospitality, leisure, travel and tourism workforce are under 25 years old (People 1st, 2006) and according to the *Labour Force Survey 2004-05*, there are over 234,000 (18 per cent) international workers employed in the sector. By far the largest sources of international workers are the Middle East and Asia, with the European workforce the second largest (31 per cent) and American and Australian workers forming the smallest proportion (8 per cent and 2 per cent respectively). International workers are likely to be young (64 per cent aged 16–39) and male (65 per cent).

Of major concern in the sector is the number of vacancies that prove hard-to-fill. The reasons for this are varied and include locality, pay and conditions, and lack of applicants with appropriate skills and experience. As illustrated in the table below, the sector experiences a higher percentage of hard-to-fill vacancies than other industries.

Table 4   *Hard-to-fill vacancies in HLT*

	Number of hard to fill vacancies		% Establishments reporting hard-to-fill vacancies	
	HLT	Whole economy	HLT (%)	Whole economy (%)
England	27,900	227,200	9	8
Scotland	3,400	33,500	11	10
Wales	n/a	n/a	15	14
N. Ireland	1,000	9,800	12	10

Source: *National Employer Skills Survey 2004*

Exploring the data on the issue of hard-to-fill vacancies reveals that the highest percentage of vacancies lies in the skilled-trade occupations and for managerial posts (see Table 5).

Table 5 Hard-to-fill vacancies as a proportion of vacancies

	Number of vacancies	Number of hard-to-fill vacancies	Hard-to-fill vacancies as a proportion of vacancies (%)
Managers	3,001	1,729	58
Associate professionals	818	184	22
Administrative/clerical staff	4,218	765	18
Skilled trades occupations	9,400	6,419	68
Personal-services staff	1,829	423	23
Sales and customer-services staff	8,272	2,655	32
Elementary staff	41,849	13,258	32

Coverage: England   Source: *National Employer Skills Survey 2004*

People 1st undertook a survey to explore why vacancies are difficult to fill and established the following reasons by occupation (2005):

Table 6 Specific reasons why occupations are hard to fill

Occupation	Reason
Chefs (fine dining – all levels)	Lack of skilled applicants
Sous chefs	Most applicants with this level of chef-skills want to be head chefs
Managers	A lack of applicants with the required skills and experience
Front of house/housekeeping	Competition from other industries, lack of public transport in rural areas
Professional roles/reception	Other sectors pay more
Tourist information staff	Lack of applicants with language skills
Housekeepers	Not enough people willing to do the job
Asian and oriental chefs	Second generation immigrants unwilling to enter industry and withdrawal of sector-based scheme (for work permits)
Food and drink service	Not enough applicants with right attitude
Casino staff	Moral reasons and shift work
Cleaners	Undesirable hours, issues with benefits

Source: People 1st working groups, 2005

Notably the reason cited for managerial positions proving difficult to fill is 'a lack of applicants with required skills and experience'. This represents a key opportunity for graduates from HE courses to fill this gap.

According to the *Labour Market Review 2000*, 17.1 per cent of the hospitality workforce had no qualifications in 1999 compared to 12.2 per cent across all industries (HTF, 2000: 45). Qualification levels continue to vary between the different employment levels in the sector as depicted in the following table.

Table 7 Qualification levels of those working in core occupations

%	NVQ Level 4 and above	NVQ Level 3 (%)	NVQ Level 2 (%)	NVQ L 1 & entry level	No qualifi- cations (%)
Hotel and accommoda- tion managers	30	19	21	14	16
Restaurant and catering managers	19	20	28	24	9
Publicans & managers licensed premises	19	24	24	20	14
Conference and exhibi- tion managers	46	21	15	12	5
Travel-agency managers	16	40	20	22	2
Chefs, cooks	7	22	32	25	14
Travel agents	19	26	27	26	2
Kitchen and catering assistants	3	14	28	34	21
Waiters, waitresses	7	27	32	20	14
Bar staff	12	30	27	20	11

Coverage: UK
Source: *Labour Force Survey 2004–05*
Base: All in employment

According to the *Labour Force Survey 2004–05*, conference and exhibition managers and hotel and accommodation managers obtain the highest level of qualifications across the industries. From an employability perspective, there are clear opportunities for graduates to carve out their careers in these, and other, categories of job in the sector.

Growth of opportunity within the HLST sectors

In the context of hospitality, AGCAS (2005: 3) reports the industry is:
> probably the world's fastest-growing, job-creating profession employing one in ten people worldwide. In the UK alone, the industry employs over 1.8 million people. It is estimated that the industry will require 30,000-35,000 trained people at management and supervisory level year on year until 2010, if it is to fulfil its potential.

Despite an increase in the number of institutions offering relevant courses identified by CHME (2005), there are reportedly too few students taking college and university courses in the relevant subject disciplines to be able to meet this growing demand. This has significant potential for those seeking to pursue a career in the sector (AGCAS, 2005: 3).

ISPAL report that leisure represents one of the fastest growing industries to-date in the 21st century. AGCAS confirm that primarily as a result of the successful 2012 London Olympics bid there are currently more graduate career opportunities in sport and leisure than ever before. Careers in sport and leisure are classified by AGCAS as falling under three broad umbrellas: health and fitness, betting and gambling; and, sport and recreation. A BASES careers guide reaffirms

> sport and exercise is not a traditional graduate industry and thus does not have
> the conventional career pathways other industries may have (2008: 14).

Essentially this means that graduates pursuing careers in these industries must adopt a more proactive approach to their own employability (BASES, 2008). There are however a multitude of exciting opportunities to pursue. In the context of tourism, Office for National Statistics figures indicate that overseas residents spent £14.3 billion in the UK in 2005 (AGCAS). The WTTC forecast the creation of 2.5 million new jobs worldwide in the year 2006 which results in a total figure yielding 2.8 per cent of the world's employment (AGCAS).

Skills sought by HLST employers

Findings from research undertaken by CHME in 2001 identified that:

> there is no evidence to suggest that graduates from hospitality management pro-
> grammes are demonstrably deficient in any of the skill areas identified by indus-
> try as important in first-line managers (CHME, 2001: 7).

Key transferable skills highlighted in the research as important for hospitality managers included: **people skills; commercial skills; transferable skills** (incorporating **both verbal and numerical ability**); and, **problem solving**. Key employability skills identified by the Institute of Hospitality are similar and include: **communication skills; interpersonal skills; team-working skills; problem solving; numeracy**; and, **IT proficiency** (AGCAS, 2007). AGCAS (2006) highlights some of the key skills for people seeking careers in food and drink as including: **ability to work under pressure, commitment**, the **ability to deliver excellence** in a fast-moving environment and **flexibility**. A similar AGCAS report on sport and leisure details essential skills as **customer service,**

communication and **teamwork**. The following table, compiled as part of the *National Employer Skills Survey 2003*, provides an indication of the skills profiles required in the hospitality, leisure, travel and tourism sector.

Table 8 Current skill profile of the sector

Skill	Level at which skill is required
Team-working skills	Across all occupations, employers feel high (or advanced) levels of team-working skills are required. They feel that managers required the highest levels of team-working skills.
Customer-handling skills	Customer-handling skills are the skills which employers are most likely to require at an advanced level, particularly amongst managers and those working in elementary occupations. There is a mixed view of the level of customer-handling skills required by those working in skilled trades which is likely to reflect the degree to which chefs interact with customers. A fifth of employers feel this skill isn't required whilst a quarter feel that this skill is required at a high level.
Communication skills	Employers believe that high levels of communication skills are needed by staff working in all occupations. High levels of communication skills are needed amongst managers and those working in elementary roles in particular. The latter are likely to be customer-facing whilst managers need high levels of communication skills to deal with both customers and staff effectively.
Management skills	Unsurprisingly, employers feel that managers are most likely to require high or advanced levels of management skills whilst those working in elementary occupations did not require these skills at all. There was a spread of views regarding those working in skilled trades. This is likely to reflect the varying managerial responsibilities of different types of chefs.
Technical and practical skills	Those working in skilled trades are most likely to require advanced levels of technical and practical skills. Managers also require high levels of these skills. The level of technical and practical skills required of those working in elementary occupations is lower with the majority of employers requiring basic or intermediate-level technical and practical skills of these staff
Numeracy skills	60 percent of employers believe that managers in the sector require high or advanced levels of numeracy skills whilst the requirement of chefs is more likely to be at the basic or intermediate level. There are differing views of the numeracy-skill requirements of those working in elementary occupations. This probably reflects the different types of occupations within this category (e.g. bar staff and gaming staff). Few employers believe that numeracy skills are not required.

Skill	Level at which skill is required.
Problem solving skills	Employers believe that the level of problem solving skills required by the workforce varies between occupations. They feel that managers are most likely to require high levels of problem solving skills whilst those working in elementary and skilled trade occupations tend to require these skills at a basic level.
Literacy skills	A similar pattern to numeracy emerges regarding literacy skill requirements with employers believing that managers need the highest level of skills. Approximately a third of employers believe that those working in elementary and skilled trade occupations only require basic levels of literacy. Few employers believe that literacy skills are not required within the workforce.
General IT user skills	The majority of employers feel that general IT user skills were not required by those working in elementary or skilled trade occupations. Of the remainder, the majority feel that only basic level IT skills are needed. There is a difference at the managerial level where the majority of employers feel that either basic or intermediate IT user skills are required.
IT professional skills	Very few employers feel that those working in elementary and skilled trade occupations need IT professional skills. Again, more employers thought that managers needed these skills but only at a basic or intermediate level.
Foreign language skills	Perhaps surprisingly, considering the sector frequently serves overseas visitors, the majority of employers feel that foreign language skills are not required amongst their workforce. Approximately 20 percent feel that managers required basic levels of foreign language skills whilst only 12 percent feel that those working in elementary occupations (frequently customer facing) need basic foreign language skills.

Coverage: England

Source: *2003 National Employer Skills Survey* http://researchtools.lsc.gov.uk/ness/home/home.asp

Base: Hospitality, leisure, travel and tourism employers

Despite a vision of what skills are required in the relevant HLST sectors, Frewin (2004) reports on claims made by People 1st, the sector skills council, that 'nearly one third of bosses in the hospitality, leisure, travel and tourism sectors say skills gaps are affecting their bottom line'. People 1st surveyed 5,800 employers identifying that more than 12,000 job vacancies remained unfilled due to candidates lacking the required skills, in particular the skills of **customer care**, **communication** and **team working**. According to *National Employer Skills Survey 2004–05*, of those hospitality, leisure, travel and tourism employers who report skills deficiencies, the most commonly cited are:

o Communication skills (64 percent)
o Team working skills (56 percent)

o   Customer handling skills (52 percent)
o   Technical and practical skills (47 percent)

Although these findings are relevant within the HLST context, they do not focus solely on graduate applicants. It is therefore important to specifically consider the demand for graduates in the sector and graduate skills more generally. In terms of 'demand', according to a CIHE (2008) investigation into what employers think and want, 86 per cent of employers rank good communication skills as important yet a majority of employers (across all industry sectors) report dissatisfaction with the ability of graduates to express themselves.

The CIHE (2008) report also highlights that the most significant 'satisfaction gap' experienced by employers is in 'commercial awareness' and 'work experience'. This is an alarming discovery when considered in light of Little and Harvey's HECSU Report findings (2006) that there has been a steady decline in the number of undergraduates taking up placements.

A 2007 Institute of Directors report notes that although research has shown that many organisations are happy with the calibre of graduates they recruit, evidence suggests that some employers find graduates can lack the generic and transferable skills critical for the workplace. A survey of their members found that 40 per cent perceived graduates unprepared for employment. A significant 90 per cent expressed the view that educational institutions should be doing more to prepare young people to enter the workplace. The top ten skills rated by IoD members as being most important for graduates to possess were:

1   Honesty and integrity
2   Basic literacy skills
3   Basic oral communication
4   Reliability
5   Being hard-working and having a good work ethic
6   Numeracy skills
7   A positive 'can do' attitude
8   Punctuality
9   The ability to meet deadlines
10 Team working and co-operation skills

When considering the generic CIHE (2008) findings from an HLST standpoint, many HLST courses offer work-based and work-related learning opportunities designed to foster levels of commercial awareness and may also provide supervised work experience opportunities. Additionally many of the skills highlighted by the Institute of Directors are addressed in the 2008 *HLST Benchmark*

Statements and the transferable skills sections of the *CIHE Student Employability Profiles* (Table 3). Despite evidence that HLST course providers are responding to the needs of the sector, there is scope to do more to foster graduate employability development.

Graduates views on employability

In 2004 Maher undertook research with graduates from hospitality management programmes to explore their perceptions of their own 'work readiness' when they entered the labour market. The survey revealed some interesting results with regard to the extent to which attributes were developed in respondents' degree programmes. Emotional intelligence is reported as being least likely to be developed whilst studying for a degree. Other attributes also attracting low percentage scores include initiative, stress tolerance and self-confidence. The following table highlights perceptions of the importance of several key attributes and the extent to which they are developed in the students' degree programmes.

Table 9 Graduate perception of employability skills and their importance

Attribute	Importance for career success (% ranking as very important or quite important)	Developed in degree programme (% ranking as developed a lot or somewhat developed)
Prioritising	97	63
Planning	91	75
Computer literacy	90	63
Commercial awareness	90	61
Decision-making	90	58
Negotiating	89	50
Teamwork	88	82
Problem-solving	87	65
Coping with ambiguity and complexity	86	39
Acting morally	84	44
Resolving conflict	80	42
Influencing	80	48
Arguing for or justifying a point of view or course of action	79	53

Ethical sensitivity	69	59
Ability to work cross-culturally	68	52
Applying subject understanding	66	69
Political sensitivity	65	34

These findings reiterate there is scope to more effectively develop of employability attributes in the HLST curriculum.

Conclusion

The HLST sector is of particular importance because of its contribution to the economy as a whole, the difficulty in recruiting and retaining candidates and, in particular, the challenge of recruiting highly skilled, managerial staff. These challenges in turn present many opportunities for qualified graduates. This chapter has provided a brief review of the current position of the HLST sector and the potential for graduates. Ross (2007) reports 'graduate recruitment remains a valuable yet relatively poorly managed recruitment segment in the international hospitality industry'. This view echoes a report by CHME (2001) which found evidence that where a graduate's skills were underutilised this could lead to their leaving their first post, and often at this point they were lost to the entire industry.

Findings from a CIHE commissioned report (2004) into employer perceptions of subject benchmarks (including HLST) highlighted that employers who responded to the survey did not have a high awareness of initiatives being undertaken in HEIs to develop students' employability skills. Although this is understandable, there is clear evidence that more must be done to work in partnership with both employers and other employability stakeholders. Graduates need to optimise their employability, HE providers need to maximise opportunities for graduates to develop their employability skills, and employers need to work in partnership with educators to ensure they are able to exploit graduate talent in order to drive the industry forward.

4

Embedding Employability in the Curriculum

In earlier chapters of this book we emphasised the growing importance of enhancing employability as a key aspect of student development and set the context for examining how HEIs are responding to the employability agenda. As Chapter 1 highlighted, while definitions of employability abound, the concept is largely associated with the development of employability attributes, career-management skills and engagement with lifelong learning. While an individual's employability can be affected by extra-curricular activities, such as voluntary and part-time work, the support that students receive through the formal curriculum influences directly their development; it is to this issue that we now turn. Educators need to be aware of the huge variety of ways in which employability can be embedded into the curriculum, so that they can select the most appropriate approaches for their own institutions and courses. This chapter focuses on how HEIs are designing curricula which enhance students' employability and several examples of successful initiatives are described.

Where do we start?

A key focus for higher education research is to explore how best to embed employability development within the curriculum. A plethora of research dedicated to employability and relevant pedagogy is being undertaken in the higher education arena. Specific recent initiatives to progress this include: Fund for the Development of Teaching and Learning (FDTL) projects; Centres for Excellence in Teaching and Learning (CETL) projects; National Teaching Fellowship

Scheme (NTFS) projects; and institutional-based research centres such as the Centre for Research and Evaluation (CRE) at Sheffield Hallam University and the Centre for Employability (CfE) at the University of Central Lancashire. In addition to these funded initiatives, extensive work is being undertaken by the Higher Education Academy (HEA) and the HEA Subject Networks. Numerous employability-related studies have been undertaken by the hospitality, leisure, sport and tourism (HLST) subject network and many relevant case studies and teaching resources can be found on the subject centre website at http://www.heacademy.ac.uk/hlst

In Scotland, much developmental research has also been undertaken on enhancing employability and this was the focus of one of the two 2004/05 Scottish Enhancement Themes which resulted in several publications and resources (see http://www.enhancementthemes.ac.uk/themes/Employability/default.asp).

The FDTL5 'Enhancing Graduate Employability' project

The Fund for the Development in Teaching and Learning (FDTL) is a HEFCE /DEL funded initiative and was established in 1995 to support projects

> aimed at stimulating developments in teaching and learning in higher educa-
> tion and to encourage the dissemination of good teaching and learning practice
> across the higher education sector.
>
> (http://www.heacademy.ac.uk/ourwork/networks/fdtl)

Since 1995, the Fund has supported 164 projects on a wide range of learning and teaching themes. One project to be funded under the fifth (and final) round of FDTL was the 'Enhancing Graduate Employability' project, managed and directed by Sarah Graves and Angela Maher at Oxford Brookes University. The project set out an ambitious plan to pilot employability initiatives in 10 institutions delivering courses in hospitality, leisure, sport and tourism (HLST). The project began in October 2004, and amongst other resources has produced a series of case studies detailing how the 10 partner institutions embedded employability into their courses. The 10 case studies are available in a sister publication to this book called *Delivering Graduate Employability: Case Studies in Hospitality, Leisure, Sport and Tourism* (Graves and Maher, 2008).

In addition, the project website contains the case studies plus a range of other employability resources, including a curriculum-audit tool developed by the project team and a comprehensive directory of employability-related materials themed under the headings of: *Employability in the Curriculum; Personal Development Planning; Work-Based and Work-Related Learning;* and *Employment and Careers* (www.enhancingemployability.org.uk). The website and its resources provide valuable information and tools for those educators interested in enhancing/embedding employability at their own institution.

Strategies for embedding employability

When institutions are thinking about how to embed employability development within the curriculum, Yorke (2006: 7) emphasises 'it is a mistake to assume that provision of experience, whether within higher education or without, is a sufficient condition for enhanced employability'. Knight and ESECT colleagues report in the *Briefings on Employability Series* that one focus should be on making the tacit, explicit. This means more than simply alerting students that certain activities in the curriculum are important for employability and instead fostering a culture of reflective practice and genuine engagement with employability related activities.

Knight (2006) notes that 'caring about good learning, teaching, assessment and curriculum is consistent with caring about enhancing student employability'. In essence employability development is synonymous with good learning. The Pedagogy for Employability Group (2004: 6) writes 'many teaching activities that promote good learning in the particular subject also promote employability in general'. In essence 'employability and subject-specific learning are complementary, not oppositional.'

When considering strategies for embedding employability in the curriculum it is important to remember there is no 'one size fits all' approach. Yorke and Knight (2006: 14) emphasise that 'contexts, student-recruitment patterns, envisaged labour markets and traditions are four variables which influence the embedding of employability in the curricula'. They highlight 'there is a spectrum of ways in which employability can be developed through the curricula' and these include four strategies:

o Employability through the whole curriculum
o Employability in the core curriculum
o Work-based or work-related learning incorporated as one or more components within the curriculum; or in parallel with the curriculum
o Employability-related module(s) within the curriculum

(Yorke and Knight, 2006: 14).

The above approaches represent 'ideal types' which may appear distinctly differentiated, however in reality there is likely to be less clear-cut delineation between strategies and some will at times overlap (Yorke and Knight, 2006). Before deciding which particular approach or combination of approaches to adopt, it is first recommended that a curriculum audit is carried out as an essential first step in understanding the institutional context into which initiatives will be developed.

The role of curriculum auditing

Yorke and Knight (2006: 11) write that:

> an intention to enhance student employability, like an intention to accustom a student to the practices that characterise a subject area, rests upon the learning, teaching and assessment methods embedded in the wider curriculum structure.

In essence both good learning and the development of employability need to be supported by commensurate approaches to learning, teaching and assessment. The technique of curriculum auditing is one which can support this coherence in curriculum design (Yorke and Knight, 2006: 11) and can help in achieving constructive alignment within programmes of study (Biggs, 1999). Undertaking an audit enables the detailed discussion and development of a particular issue. The technique of curriculum audit is gaining popularity for embedding employability development and a range of tools are available to facilitate the process. The Higher Education Academy Centre for Bioscience has produced an Employability Audit which is defined as having a *developmental* purpose, and

> not simply to come up with an overall score for the course. It is designed to help teachers *consider* the content and design of a course with respect to the issue of *employability* and to see where they could improve the course to better address the issue.

The Employability Audit tool can be found in Appendix 2 and further copies can be downloaded from: http://www.bioscience.heacademy.ac.uk/resources/audit. aspx. It is an extremely valuable way of helping educators to reflect on their current practices as regards employability and can be a powerful staff-development tool. It asks educators to consider issues such as their knowledge about graduates' employment outcomes (and their knowledge of the labour-market opportunities), their relationships with employers, career-management-skills development and whether the curriculum promotes employability.

Having undertaken an audit to consider some of the broader issues, a further useful tool to facilitate a more focused curriculum audit is offered by the FDTL 'Enhancing Graduate Employability' project team (http://www.enhancingemployability.org.uk/files_adhoc/curriculum_audit_instrument.doc).   This instrument encourages staff to review their courses in detail by considering the promotion of learner autonomy, development of skills (including career-management skills), Personal Development Planning (PDP), and the contribution that work-based and work-related learning can make to skills development and work-awareness.

Embedding employability through the whole curriculum: the case of PDP

Employability through the whole curriculum is perhaps the most ambitious strategy in which a set of 'transferable' skills or competencies are integrated through an entire programme (Yorke and Knight, 2004). Possibly one of the best known and 'purest' examples of this approach is in operation at Alverno College in the USA where students are required to demonstrate evidence of achievement in eight broad 'abilities' including communication, analysis, problem solving, decision-making and social interaction. Tutor feedback is provided on level of achievement but students' work is not formally graded (see details on the college website at http://www.alverno.edu/about_alverno/ability_curriculum.html). Although in no way as radical as the Alverno model, parallels may be drawn with numerous examples in the UK of university-wide approaches to embedding of transferable skills in the curriculum. The UK examples do employ traditional assessment/grading methods and also tend to steer away from explicit reference to abilities such as 'effective citizenship' and 'aesthetic responsiveness' used at Alverno.

The University of Luton is one example of an institution in the UK which has undertaken a university-wide initiative to embedding a set of skills across all undergraduate courses. Although longitudinal evaluative data regarding the impact of the Luton skills initiative is not available, less formal evidence suggests a correlation between the initiative and a positive effect on student performance (Atlay and Harris, 2000; Fallows and Steven, 2000). More recently, the introduction of Personal Development Planning (PDP) in HE institutions in the UK offers the opportunity to integrate generic competencies across and within programmes, although the extent to which this happens in practice depends very much on the individual approach adopted by a particular institution. The sheer volume of advice and case studies on PDP is overwhelming and there are many examples of how PDP is being implemented in different institutions, from institutional policy frameworks for PDP to designing specific PDP modules (see the HEA website for example http://www.heacademy.ac.uk/ourwork/learning/pdp?page=1 for advice and resources). Discussion of PDP is closely aligned with issues of student *reflection* and *planning* and discourse in this area:

emphasises the importance of improving students' understanding of how they are learning, of offering students an opportunity to develop a holistic overview of their course, of enabling students to reflect critically and become more independent, as well as encouraging students to consider actively their academic, extracurricular activity and career opportunities (Clegg, 2004: 289).

There is a good deal of evidence to suggest that PDP has a positive effect. Based on an extensive literature review of teaching interventions, Gough et al (2003) concluded that PDP had positive effects on student learning, student attainment, and approaches to learning (although Gough admitted it was not possible to know 'how or why' PDP was producing those effects reported – Clegg, 2004). In terms of specific case studies on embedding employability in the curriculum at a school-wide level, staff at the University of Paisley in the School of Media, Language and Music worked to integrate PDP into the core curriculum. They adopted an integrated approach to curriculum design which 'placed employability for creative and cultural industries at the top of the organising hierarchy for programme frameworks' (Gifford and Robertson, 2005). Details of this and many other case studies can be downloaded from the Scottish Employability Quality Enhancement Theme website at http://www.enhancementthemes.ac.uk/themes/Employability/publications.asp.

Within the context of the FDTL 'Enhancing Graduate Employability' project conducted by the authors, one case study in particular focuses explicitly on the relationship between PDP and employability. Students studying sport at the University of Ulster have been asked to use the university's PDP system to help them audit and assess their employability skills and to identify 'gaps' in their skills base. This information is then used by students, in discussion with course tutors, to help them compile action plans for how they might enhance and develop their skills during an (optional) placement year or in their final year of study (Brennan and Murphy, 2008).

The second series of the *Learning and Employability* publications produced by the Higher Education Academy contains a resource entitled *Personal Development Planning and Employability* (Ward et al, 2006). This publication, by Rob Ward and colleagues, offers guidance on embedding PDP practice in the curriculum, supporting and assessing personal development, developing PDP to support employability from an institutional perspective and it also contains a range of practical case studies.

PDP is thought to impact positively on employability and is more likely to be effective if integrated into the curriculum and supported by academic staff (HEA

2005a). PDP can also help students understand how to evidence their learning and achievements to employers and can help them develop their career-management skills through engaging them with processes of CPD early in their career (HEA 2005b). The process of PDP is seen by employers to be of great value and graduate recruiters believe it is both good preparation for recruitment as well as fostering a structured reflective developmental approach to learning (Lees, 2002).

Embedding employability in the core curriculum

Embedding employability through the core curriculum involves the identification of a finite number of modules (usually compulsory) in which to embed development of a set of employability skills. This approach is arguably easier to implement than employability through the whole curriculum, particularly within large, diverse institutions and those which offer flexible modular programmes (Yorke and Knight, 2004). The University of Luton case study cited in the previous section required that each programme of study designate two modules (one each at Levels 5 and 6) as vehicles for the formal development of the 'transferable skills', thus ensuring employability was located in the core of all curricula. Further informative case studies on embedding employability in universities are available at the website http://www.heacademy.ac.uk/resources/detail/ourwork/tla/employability_tools_case_studies which includes examples of initiatives undertaken by London Metropolitan University, Sheffield Hallam University, University of Exeter and University of Glamorgan, among others.

There are several case studies within the FDTL 'Enhancing Graduate Employability' project which have explored this approach. For example, the University of Bolton study sought to embed employability development within specific core modules at Levels 4, 5 and 6 (Snape, 2008). This approach is driven in part by the need to implement the university's standard PDP framework but recognises the need for contextualising learning for undergraduate programmes in sport, leisure and tourism management. The research at Bolton also explores the effectiveness of this approach on student perceptions and attitudes of their employability using questionnaires, and focuses on helping students articulate and provide evidence for their skills using written learning records.

The Department of Leisure, Tourism and Hospitality at the University of Gloucestershire is also exploring the impact of embedding employability in the core curriculum. Having identified the skills of reflection and reflective writing as being important in the context of employability and personal development, the department has embedded activities into their core Level 4, 5 and 6 modules to progressively foster student development (Buswell and Tomkins, 2008). Of particular note in Gloucester's case study is the use of the technique of storytelling at Level 6 to encourage deep reflection and to help students make sense of complex experiences which occur during their work placement (Danto, 1985; McDury and Alterio, 2003). Other activities in the core programme include the completion of a personal skills audit, authoring of a reflective portfolio, in addition to the use of critical narrative post-placement.

Employability-related modules within the curriculum

A further approach to embedding employability involves the development of specific employability-related modules such as personal skills development and career planning. This again may represent a more practical approach to embedding employability skills development and is a popular method within the HE sector. While some approaches such as that at Alverno outlined earlier are clearly more ambitious, research by Yorke and Knight (2004) indicates that much is to be gained by small-scale 'tweaking' of the curriculum. As long as the 'tweaking' process is managed effectively this approach has great potential to make an impact on students' claims to be employable, and it is possibly much more attractive to educators who eschew a more fundamental reworking of the curriculum.

Examples of skills-oriented modules at the beginning of study programmes can be found in Abramson and Jones (2001) and Booth (2001). However it is important to recognise that skills development should be embedded within study programmes, not 'bolted on' or 'boxed off' from the rest of the curriculum. Yorke and Knight (2003: 15) cite the example of Haigh and Kilmartin (1999):

> in providing an evaluation of the first-year Geography curriculum at Oxford Brookes University, describe the integration of 'personal transferable skills' within a pedagogic approach based on active learning, and in which there are no lectures.

Another example is Napier University which has developed a 'generic bridging module' worth 15 module credits. This module is designed to facilitate student transition from school to higher education and specifically to enhance their study skills and employability skills during the course (Godfrey, 2005). A very useful publication of case studies undertaken as part of the Scottish Enhancement project is also evaluated in Macfarlane-Dick and Roy (2006).

There are many examples of employability-related modules within curricula across all disciplines and these may include modules based around:

o   entrepreneurship and enterprise skills

o   career planning and career management skills
o   reflective practice modules
o   work-based consultancy or research projects.

Included under the category of employability-related modules is the freestanding curricular provision which supports career planning and job search strategies. Yorke and Knight (2003: 15) state that:

> In many cases a preferred way of enhancing an institution's contribution to student employability is to strengthen the careers service, although the impact will be muted if the service lacks a curriculum presence.

This message reinforces the point that such provision needs to be embedded into the curriculum and not merely 'bolted on' to courses. An example of an institution-wide initiative is Reading University which requires students on all undergraduate programmes to undertake a compulsory *Career Management Skills* module worth five credits (the module can also be embedded into modules of 10 or 20 credits) This is a bold move by a university, but one which demonstrates considerable commitment to enhancing employability and Reading has won several national awards for the module (http://www.reading.ac.uk/).

One research case study undertaken as part of the FDTL 'Enhancing Graduate Employability' project involved the piloting of a module entitled *Developing Your Management Skills* (Martin and McCabe, 2008). This module is aimed at postgraduate hospitality and tourism students and designed to help them develop career management skills, drawing explicitly on students' part-time work experiences, which the researchers identified as an increasingly common aspect of life at Sheffield Hallam University. An interesting aspect of this case study is its focus on postgraduate students who are mostly international in origin. At Oxford Brookes University employability is being embedded via a compulsory first-year module in which skills are evaluated and assessed using, amongst other techniques, a card-sort exercise which focuses attention on what employers want and what makes employees successful at work (Whittaker, 2008).

As a further exemplar, work is also being undertaken at Oxford Brookes University on a final year career-planning module for undergraduate hospitality and tourism students (Maher, 2008). The module is at honours level and is compulsory for those students on sandwich programmes. Students are required to engage in a range of self-assessment/diagnostic activities to develop understanding of their work values, employability skills and career aspirations. Students are also required to undertake a detailed analysis of the labour market and to evaluate the research on graduate skills. The final part of the module incorporates workshops to develop key skills such as networking, interviewing, CV writing and time management. The module also incorporates a mock-assessment centre held off campus at a local hotel and facilitated by professional human-resources managers from industry. The module assignment comprises a portfolio containing a critical review of the literature on the labour market and demand for graduate skills, a reflective commentary/evaluation of their own employability skills (supported by appropriate evidence) and a ten-year career plan. An employer-mentoring programme will form part of the module in 2008–09 and Oxford Brookes has signed up 50 employer mentors representing all sectors of hospitality and tourism to support students in their career planning.

Work-based or work-related modules within/parallel with the curriculum

Work-based learning (WBL) and work-related learning (WRL) are curriculum strategies most commonly associated with enhancing employability. A definition of WBL is:

> learning in the workplace, derived from work undertaken for or by an employer (i.e. in paid or unpaid work). It involves the gaining of competencies and knowledge in the workplace (CIHE, 2005: 2).

Boud and Solomon (2003: 4) state that WBL is 'the term being used to describe a class of university programmes which bring together universities and work organisations to create new learning opportunities in work places'. Engagement with WBL is widely reported to positively impact on student employability, and a period of work experience is aligned closely with the possession of many skills essential for success at work (Little and Harvey, 2006).

WRL is in turn about 'making graduates ready and able to make the transition from education to the workplace', defined specifically as 'learning outcomes achieved through activities which are based in, or derive from, the context of work or the workplace' (Hills et al, 2003). Examples of WRL include field trips, 'live' case studies, consultancy type assignments and projects, and employer involvement in teaching and assessment (Moreland, 2006). Litteljohn and Watson (2004) reiterate that in developing graduate managers for hospitality and tourism it is important to embrace both work-based and work-related learning aspects but also stress that there is no one best way to facilitate the development of highly employable graduates.

WBL opportunities can be organised in different ways and these are summarised by Little et al (2006):

Organised work experience as part of a programme of study
This would include a compulsory or optional work placement as part of a conventional course, generic 'work experience' modules available to students on a range of programmes or work experience through a programme wholly or predominantly delivered in the workplace.

Organised work experience external to a programme of study
This includes national programmes such as the Careers Research and Advisory Centre's (CRAC) InsightPlus which helps students recognise skills they develop during part-time or voluntary employment (www.insightplus.co.uk) and STEP Enterprise which organises for second-year undergraduates to work (usually during the summer vacation) in small companies and not-for-profit organisations (www.step.org.uk). In addition there are local schemes run by single or university partnerships (e.g. the 'York Award', 'Business Bridge' run by three Liverpool Universities, and Sheffield Plus)

Ad hoc work experience external to a programme of study
This includes work experience (paid or unpaid) which is not planned at the outset as part of a taught programme, nor is it 'organised' in the sense of the schemes mentioned above. Term-time working is increasing with almost 60 per cent of undergraduates undertaking part-time work while studying (Callender and Wilkinson, 2003)

Work experience itself is not necessarily intrinsically beneficial. However, there is considerable evidence that good work experience opportunities, if well managed, are educationally very valuable and can greatly enhance a student's employability, and their employment opportunities (Knight and Yorke, 2004). Harvey and Bowes (1999) found that students undertaking sandwich degrees were much more likely to be in full-time employment six months after graduating (70 per cent sandwich compared with 55 per cent full time courses). Harvey and Blackwell (1999) in a separate study of art and design students also found that graduates with some form of work experience were significantly more likely to be in full-time permanent employment than those who undertook no work experience during their studies. The authors also state that graduates with relevant work experience were more likely to have operated their own business since graduating, to be more entrepreneurial, than other art and design graduates, and were less likely to have been unemployed.

Several case studies have taken place under the umbrella of the FDTL 'Enhancing Graduate Employability' project which focus on WBL or WRL. The research conducted at Liverpool John Moores University set up a WBL forum consisting of employers, lecturers and students which draws together the views of these key stakeholders 'to produce a curriculum structure that transfers students' employability potential into reality' (Beattie, Nixon and Walker, 2008). The partnership aspect of this case study is critical to developing a curriculum which is effective in developing 'highly employable graduates'. City College Norwich (Hingley, 2008) and Westminster Kingsway College (Sheehan and Waghorn, 2008) case studies also research aspects of employer engagement and mentoring as a means of enhancing students' employability, whereas case studies undertaken at Leeds Metropolitan (Jameson, 2008) and the University of Worcester (Bill, 2008) focus on work placement and entrepreneurship respectively.

Many case studies are also available from the Higher Education Academy and Subject Centre websites which detail practical examples of the development of work-based and work-related learning modules. As just one example, the HLST website contains a case study focusing on industry-education links at Manchester Metropolitan University. The featured module entitled *'Live' Group Enterprise Projects* is:

> a unit designed to enhance industry and educational links within hospitality
> and tourism education and to develop students' intrapersonal and interpersonal
> management skills and competencies (Ineson, 2005).

Students have the opportunity to engage in live consultancy projects with industry while receiving guidance from academic staff. In Scotland, the Aberdeen Business School at Robert Gordon University report on a mentoring scheme established for postgraduates students undertaking an MSc in HRM. Connon, Stevenson and Cruickshank (2005) report:

> the aim of the scheme is to ease the transition from being a student in tertiary
> education to working in an HR professional role and thereby enhancing the
> students' employability.

Conclusion

The above examples represent several of the many approaches adopted and documented around the country to facilitate student development and serve as exemplars of the multitude of strategies available for embedding employability in the curriculum. An awareness of the changing labour market and the needs of employers cited above must permeate higher education (Harvey et al, 1997). While work experience has proven valid at enhancing student employability (Dearing 1997; DfEE, 1998; Little and Harvey, 2006), it is fundamental for educationalists to think beyond solely work-based learning interventions and embrace different strategies. Other innovative ways to embed employability skills development within curricula are being tried across the HE sector, from simple employability card sorts to complex PDP portfolios which demonstrate student development across a range of activities and over the entire period of their studies.

The development of employability attributes is of particular relevance for subject areas like hospitality, leisure, sport and tourism (HLST), given the challenges to be faced and the type of roles graduates are likely to pursue (see Chapter 3). While many higher education institutions are incorporating the development of employability skills into their curricula using a number of strategies, it would seem there is still some way to go before the HE sector can be said to be addressing employability on a level par with other aspects of teaching, learning and assessment. The final chapter of this book examines this latter issue alongside others that will need to be tackled if enhancing employability is to be taken seriously as part of curriculum processes in HE.

5

Enhancing Graduate Employability
Can Higher Education Deliver?

Previous chapters in this book have highlighted a whole range of issues relating to enhancing the employability of students in HE. It is clear that government in Britain (and around the world) is concerned that HEIs focus on the development of graduates' employability so that they can make the greatest possible contribution to 'human capital' and economic growth (Yorke and Knight, 2007; DIUS, 2008). However, it is also clear from a review of the literature and research on employability that responses from HEIs have been highly variable, both in terms of attitudes towards the employability agenda and in approaches to embedding employability in institutional practices. This chapter addresses some key issues which require further scrutiny if enhancing employability is to be delivered effectively across the HE sector.

An institution-wide view
Conceptual clarification and terminology
Much of the debate surrounding employability can be put down to a lack of consensus about what employability actually means. Conceptually, employability is open to a range of interpretations and definitions and there is often a blurring of the distinction between **employment** (i.e. having a job) and **employability** (possessing attributes which facilitate and enhance job opportunities). There is also much uneasiness about the language of employability and the use of the term 'skills' has met with particular hostility in many areas of academia.

However, it has been argued (quite convincingly) by advocates of enhancing employability that debate over meanings and language have merely served to distract attention from the fact that employability enhancement is synonymous with 'good learning' and not in any way in competition with developing subject knowledge. Knight and Yorke (2000) argue that the development of skills such as communication, literacy, numeracy, teamwork and learning how to learn – seen as key employability skills – are just as valuable purely on educational grounds and can enhance students' performance on their courses. Indeed enhancing employability is closely aligned with many higher-level skills and cognitive abilities (critical thinking, analytic abilities, assimilating complex data, etc). Teaching methods for a particular subject may assist students to develop key and other skills – and development of key skills (e.g. use of IT for information retrieval) will facilitate learning of the subject. So it can be seen as a two-way dialogue between subject and skills (Yorke, 2001).

Knight and Yorke (2001) also argue that employability can be embedded in any academic subject in HE without compromising core academic freedoms:

> Employability is more than about developing attributes, techniques or experience just to enable a student to get a job, or to progress within a current career. It is about learning and the emphasis is less on 'employ' and more on 'ability'. In essence, the emphasis is on developing critical, reflective abilities, with a view to empowering and enhancing the learner. Employment is a by-product of this enabling process (Harvey, 2003: 3).

There is no doubt that employability is a complex construct which goes well beyond the boundaries of 'key skills' and similar terms:

> It sits at the conjunction of a number of discourses that include the subject discipline(s) studied; both individual and social psychology; communication; organisational sociology; and perhaps elements of management and finance (Yorke and Knight, 2003: 19).

Be this as it may, our understanding of employability and how to enhance it have come a long way in the past 15 or 20 years and there is much research evidence to suggest certain approaches work well. Attention may need to be paid to encouraging staff to engage in discussion and dialogue about employability and some of the research and tools developed and freely available in the academic community via the HEA website could be useful here. The Employability Audit tool produced by the Bioscience Subject Network (see Appendix 2) offers a practical starting point for raising issues relating to students employability. Even if it generates disagreement initially, at least it will open up debate.

Universities also need to consider their approach to incorporating employability into institutional practices. Employability is itself a concept which is both complex and politically charged and attempts by senior management to implement a top-down approach to embedding employability could be seen as an attack on academic freedom. Change is more likely to stick if it is led from the 'bottom up', especially in the 'anarchy of individualism that is academia' (Lees, 2002: 5). All commentators concur that staff need to 'own' the changes which are being proposed and that little can be achieved without staff commitment to the agreed change. Atlay and Harris (2000) believe that organisational culture is critical in the successful implementation of change, and change will happen more easily in an institution which genuinely strives to improve its learning environment for the benefit of students and staff.

While there is little likelihood of a move away from the use of the terminology of 'skills' when discussing employability, academics and students may be more open to the use of terms such as 'graduate attributes' and 'graduate capability' which are increasingly apparent in the literature. The notion of 'capability' (Stephenson, 1998) captures much of the breadth of perspective on employability in its assertion of the desirability that a graduate should – in brief – become an effective operator in the world (whether in employment or other social setting) (Yorke et al, 2003: 19). Whatever the terminology, it has become increasingly apparent that both students and government are expecting universities to do much more in terms of enhancing the employability of graduates and pressure is only likely to increase as education becomes more expensive and accountable.

Measuring success: employability performance indicators

One key aspect of employability is knowing when one has been successful – how does an institution know that it is effectively enhancing the employability of its graduates? Once again this is a complex issue. Generally accepted measures of employability used by universities and reported to government focus on the numbers of graduates getting jobs. However, this approach to measuring employability of graduates has many problems (aside from confusing employability with employment) and may need to be reviewed if universities are to be encouraged to take seriously the enhancing of employability. Firstly, using raw statistics on graduates in employment does not take into account the level (quality) of the job (i.e. whether graduates are employed in suitably demanding work) nor does it take into account the diversity of graduate employment.

If one measure of success is the 'quality' of graduates then Little (2001) questions whether graduate employment figures are in any way trustworthy indicators of the quality of HE. Using first destination return statistics (FDR) as the basis for compiling data on graduate employment has inherent weaknesses as data is gathered six months after graduation when many students will be travelling or still looking for work. The survey does not distinguish between those who are not looking for work and those who are unintentionally unemployed. Such data should be treated with caution, yet it is often taken at face value by prospective students, parents and other key stakeholders. This is a difficult area for HEIs, yet it is an important one to highlight, as employment statistics are increasingly being used as a key measure of a universities performance. Data on graduate employment is publicly available and published in league tables, thus creating the impression that some universities better prepare their students for employment.

While the weaknesses are recognised there have been few studies on better alternatives. Harvey (2000) and Smith et al (2000) have proposed that universities construct performance indicators based on individual student data – using a combination of FDR data matched to administrative data on individual student records, e.g. subject of study, gender, age, ethnicity, occupation of parents, entry qualification. Harvey also suggests that FDR data should be collected at least one year after graduation or as time-series data for each cohort (although he does recognise that data collection may be more problematic the longer the graduate is out of university). Such measures are more sophisticated and would provide some measure of quality as it would ascertain the added-value of undertaking a university course. However, it is likely that many universities would consider the collection and analysis of such complex data too onerous a task.

The introduction of any Employability Performance Indicator (EPI) needs to be considered very carefully as there is a danger that this will be economically-driven and used for accountability purposes if based solely on numbers in employment. Given the public nature of employment statistics, institutions may be tempted to manipulate the data as they seek to improve their position in the league tables. Harvey (2000a) stresses that the EPI must have greater emphasis on 'improvement' (rather than accountability) and be focused on internal development and quality improvement – and should clearly be used as part of the institutional learning process. However as Lees (2002: 10) points out:

> there is considerable pressure from the government and funding agencies to 'keep employability simple', so employability is being *de facto* equated to the gaining and retaining of work.

An alternative measure of success: the curriculum audit

If employability is defined in broader terms (i.e. attributes of the graduate) and development seen as a process (as opposed to a product) of education then institutional effectiveness might be indicated by means of an audit (Harvey, 2000a; 2001). The audit would identify developmental opportunities within the institution such as work-experience and other employability enhancing options available within the curriculum. Harvey (2000a) argues that league tables do not offer an institution guidelines for finding gaps in its provision or where it might make improvements or progress in enhancing employability, whereas an audit would help in this way. This type of approach to 'measuring' effectiveness lies clearly within the philosophy of understanding employability as a process, and fostering organisational learning.

Institutional responsibility for employability

It is clear from research conducted into employability that support from senior management within an institution can be critical in embedding enhancement initiatives. The literature suggests that enhancement of graduate employability should be seen as a strategic issue and institutions need to establish how they would like to communicate their commitment, what employability means and also how they will judge institutional success. Knight and Yorke (2004) suggest that an institutional approach would involve the following:

Undertake groundwork

Research to establish how various constituencies in the university construe employability and how it is currently being tackled, in order to establish what developmental work needs to be undertaken.

Establish an implementation team

Innovations require all parts of the institution to be engaged and the implementation team needs to be chosen carefully so that all interests are seen to be represented.

Communicate well

The institution needs to decide on language that is relatively straightforward (avoiding use of employability/bureaucratic 'jargon') and to adopt a communication strategy which allows institutional members to be involved in developing the approach to employability.

Develop a shared commitment

This means allowing and encouraging 'ownership' and recognising the autonomy of academic staff, while striking a balance with a coherent set of broad institutional expectations.

Generate some early successes

Adopting a 'low cost, high gain' approach by 'tweaking' curricula can be of great benefit in a context where staff feel hard-pressed. Tweaking may involve making minor changes such as the introduction of a placement year or the embedding of a career management module, and publicising these early successes – the key however is to **embed** and **consolidate**, not to 'bolt on' such practices.

Much can be learned about successful implementation of employability from the Skills *Plus* project and the pilot projects conducted as part of it (Knight and Yorke, 2000; 2003; 2004). However there is a clear message to take from the outcomes of the project; that institutional support at the highest level is a prerequisite to success:

> commitment to employability has to be associated with sufficient institutional sponsorship if it is to be taken seriously. This does not mean that a senior academic has to be the 'institutional expert' on employability, but rather that such a person has to understand enough about what it implies to take the role of institutional champion (and the role has to be sustained if it is to be effective) in respect of development and implementation (Knight and Yorke, 2004: 203).

A programme and curriculum view

While there may be good institutional direction and support for the embedding of employability, there are still many issues to address at departmental and curriculum level in choosing effective ways of enhancing students' skills in this area. Some key issues are discussed below.

The status of employability in the curriculum: education versus training

Employability is seen by some as 'skills' training, and therefore not on a par with learning academic subject disciplines. This can impact negatively on the development of employability as there may be a tendency to ignore employability altogether in the formal curriculum, or to 'bolt on' some work experience or career management development opportunities. In more extreme cases anything to do with employability may be 'farmed out' to the university Careers Centre and employability never referred to in the student's course.

Much of the material presented so far in this book has argued that enhancement of employability is equally as important as subject knowledge in the overall development of the student – and employability should be seen as part of the student's 'entitlement' at university. While a minority of employers may complain that graduates are not always 'work-ready', they are also very clear that they do not want 'trained' recruits. Employers insist that they are seeking:

> intelligent, rounded people who have a depth of understanding, can apply themselves, take responsibility and develop their role in the organisation. Employers want graduate recruits who are educated and can demonstrate a wide range of attributes, not least the traditional high-level academic abilities of analysis, reflection, critique and synthesis. Employers do not want graduates trained for a job, not least because jobs change rapidly (Harvey, 2003: 6).

Rapid and continuous changes in organisational structures, strategies and operations, alongside a global information revolution and the need to be responsive to the needs of customers and other stakeholders underlines the necessity for graduates who are adaptive and have a high degree of 'practical intelligence'. Practical intelligence requires the use of tacit knowledge which is:

> the procedural knowledge one learns in everyday life that is usually not taught and often is not even verbalised. Tacit knowledge includes things like knowing what to say to whom, knowing when to say it, and knowing how to say it for maximum effect (Sternberg and colleagues, 2000: ix).

Tacit knowledge, they argue, is even more important given the pace of change in employer organisations over the last twenty years.

Skills development in the curriculum

While it is tempting to simplify employability into a list of skills which can be taught or delivered as part of a programme, the reality is much more complex. Employability interacts with a whole range of discourses and touches on many different disciplines. To try and reduce it to a simple list of skills would be misleading. However, the notion of skills (and the skills lists presented in chapters 2 and 3) should not be totally ignored as they represent important indicators, or signifiers, of student achievement and capability.

As outlined in Chapter 1, the USEM model provides a useful way of thinking about employability and there is considerable empirical evidence to suggest it has high face validity and is consistent with academic values. The interplay of understanding, skilful practices, efficacy beliefs and metacognition are central to understanding employability and the complex learning it entails. However, the model needs to be taken from its current level of abstraction for it to be useful in curriculum design. Knight and Yorke (2004) in their book *Learning, Curriculum and Employability in Higher Education* offer detailed advice on the embedding of employability using the USEM model (based on both research and empirical evidence of what works). A brief recap on USEM may be useful at this stage:

Understanding

Students need to remember relevant facts, to understand concepts, to apply their understandings in different contexts (both familiar and unfamiliar), to have the ability to analyse and critically evaluate materials (e.g. literature) or situations. Subject knowledge is incorporated into 'understanding'.

Skilful practices

The procedural knowledge needed for the deployment of disciplinary expertise – often labelled under 'soft' skills and highly visible in many of the lists of skills in earlier chapters (e.g. self-management, ability to work productively with others, ability to deal with conflict, etc). Often equated to knowing 'how' as opposed to knowing 'what'.

Efficacy beliefs

Is about the student's self-theory. Malleable self-theories go with a disposition to see tasks as opportunities for learning, rather than as performance-oriented opportunities to show competence. Efficacy has a long research pedigree and is linked to (among others): self theories (Dweck, 1999); emotional intelligence (Goleman, 1996); self-efficacy (Bandura, 1997); locus of control (Rotter, 1966) and practical intelligence (Sternberg, 1997). Persistence, self-confidence and belief that one can make a difference are all associated with efficacy and to a person's capacity to develop.

Metacognition

Also has an established literature and has three interrelated aspects: knowing what you know (strategic thinking), knowing how it can be used (applicability to the task at hand) and knowing how you get to new 'knowings' (personal self-awareness) (Knight and Yorke, 2003; 2004). The more aware students are of what they know and how they know, the better able they will be to use resources to good effect. Knowledge of one's own strengths and weaknesses and self-reflection are critical elements of metacognition.

In short, Knight and Yorke (2004) advocate that programmes need to apply USEM to develop an 'employability-aware' curriculum which contains 'employ-ability-enhancing' practices. Chapter 4 covered some good examples of developing **employability-aware curricula** (i.e. employability through the whole curriculum; employability on the core curriculum; work-based or work-related learning in parallel with the curriculum and employability related modules in the curriculum). In designing 'employability-aware' curricula it is critical that students' learning experiences are coherent and progressive, and that such curricula foster learning cultures to help students understand what they are learning and why they are learning it. 'Knowing students' are those who appreciate how their employability is being developed and know how the learning, teaching and assessment activities relate to its different elements.

Curriculum development for employability will take time (months and years) and will take practice (trial and error). Students need to hear repeatedly what they should be learning and ideally programme-level planning would take priority over individual module planning (Yorke et al, 2003). Complex learning takes years and departments will need to allow for experimentation and continuous redevelopment, refinement and improvement of their approaches, especially in the early days. Employability will only succeed in a department where skills are widely valued, by both students and faculty, and where students are encouraged and able to take responsibility for evidencing their achievements. A key objective of the curriculum will be to develop all four aspects of USEM and to emphasise that all four matter equally.

Providing opportunities for developing employability

Chapter 4 has already provided many examples of 'employability-enhancing practices' and we want to revisit two of the most popular 'practices' here; work-based learning and PDP.

Work-based and work-related learning: working with employers

Learning from work is a key area which has received much attention and is perhaps one of the most obvious ways that students' employability can be enhanced. Almost all recent employer surveys specify the importance of this type of learning (CBI, 2008; CIHE, 2008; DIUS, 2008) and this approach is also keenly endorsed by academics (see for example; Little and Harvey, 2006; Nixon et al, 2006; Boud and Solomon, 2001; Brennan and Little, 1996; Bourner and Ellerker, 1994).

Work placement that is well managed and encourages students to reflect on their learning is highly valued. Students themselves also value work placement as an opportunity to develop key skills and to enable them to make good 'claims' to employability. The majority of placement students report personal and intellectual development, as well as increased levels of confidence and enhanced motivation towards study. (Little and Harvey, 2007). Despite the resounding support for WBL and placement, Little and Harvey (2006 and 2007: 227) report:

a decline in the numbers of UK students taking up placements, and [their] study suggests that more general moves towards flexibility within undergraduate programmes may be contributing to this decline.

Sandwich programmes are generally in decline and where students are undertaking work placement they are spending shorter period in work. Brennan and Tang (2008) also found that fewer UK students receive work experience through placement compared to the EU average and that UK graduates say they feel less prepared for work after graduation. Reasons for the decline can be categorised into three broad areas:

Lack of placement opportunities

Too few employers offering work placement opportunities or too much competition for placements in a particular geographical area.

Lack of take-up by students

International students particularly may want to spend three rather than four years at university and the increase in mature students may mean that they may be less mobile due to family/other commitments.

Cost

For the students, another year at university may mean more debt (although UK placements are usually paid), and institutions may perceive WBL and placements to be expensive to organise and administer.

Given the importance and value placed on work experience it is rather alarming to note this decline, both in opportunities for, and take up of, placement. If the benefits of work experience are to be realised both education and employers may need to work harder to provide possibilities for learning from work. Although many students work part-time during their studies, this is not seen to be as high-value as structured and supervised work placements that encourage depth of reflection and provide a sustained time period in which to learn and develop. It is important to weigh up carefully the benefits of WBL and WRL for students' employability and to commit appropriate time, effort and resources to ensure it works well.

Personal Development Planning: providing opportunities to reflect

Progress files represent a major policy initiative involving the use of Personal Development Planning (PDP). PDP has strong claims to enhancing the employability of students and there has been widespread take-up of PDP across the university sector. PDP has been implemented in a huge variety of ways in different institutions (Edwards, 2005; Ward and colleagues, 2006; see also chapter 4) and is aimed at the production of autonomous learners who are capable of planning for their own career and personal futures (Clegg, 2004). Although there are many claims that PDP does improve students learning (see Gough et al, 2003) Clegg argues 'that "evidence" of 'what works' is unlikely to yield useful knowledge for practitioners as long as this evidence is based on untheorised accounts of PDP' (2004: 287).

She is particularly concerned by the way the term **reflection** is used with little consistency or taking account of any cultural variation. Reflection is a highly complex concept and yet Clegg argues it is often treated very simplistically in the PDP literature and guidance on implementing PDP. It follows that this may translate into rather simplistic PDP practices. The fact that reflection is such a difficult concept has led some institutions to prefer to use the term 'review'. Clegg (2004: 292) states:

> It is interesting to note that in some places the term 'reflection' is being replaced by the seemingly more neutral term 'review' (LTSN Generic Centre, 2003b) in recognition that, in some discipline areas and for some students and teachers, reflection may suggest a discourse with which practitioners are not comfortable. The attempt to domesticate the concept of reflective and remove it from its critical epistemological moorings in order to make it more palatable; however, does not address the problems identified in the critical literature.

PDP, in fact, seems to have become one of the more unpopular aspects of educational policy in recent times and has been given a 'lukewarm reception' by both academics and students. Academic staff claim that they have more important things to do than wade through complex documentation (Wright & Knight, 2000) and students complain that the curriculum is already overloaded and can't see the point of yet more work.

There are obvious issues which must be addressed if PDP is to become an effective part of the educative process, and it is beyond the scope of this book to tackle this in detail here. Suffice to say that PDP could provide a vehicle for both reflection and articulation of employability but, in order to do this effectively, it needs to be applied in a way which genuinely develops the students ability to be autonomous and develop the capability to reflect – if it merely allows students to 'mimic' reflection then it will in all likelihood continue to be resisted by those in HE.

Assessing employability

The final issue to address is the assessment of students' employability attributes. This is an area which has taxed even the most ardent supporters of employability;

and has been used by detractors as a reason why employability cannot/should not be addressed in the curriculum. Assessment is a critically important aspect of HE and its value in directing students' approaches to study should not be underestimated. Assessment affects how students study and can encourage them to take a 'deep' rather than a 'surface' approach to learning (Entwhistle, 1996). Assessment criteria also inform students of what they need to improve upon to succeed, and identify what their tutors perceive to be important. For assessment to be meaningful however students need to understand what and why they are being asked to do it:

> If students see an assessment task as essentially just a hoop to be jumped through, with no relevance or importance to them beyond passing the assessment, the re-search suggests that they are likely to take a surface approach (Rust, 2002: 150).

Rust suggests therefore that assessment tasks work best when they are related to real-world issues. This would seem to set a good basis for the assessment of employability.

However assessment of employability is very difficult because of the nature of the 'achievements' involved. How does one assess self-efficacy or emotional intelligence? Many of the skills listed as valued employability attributes in chapters 2 and 3 would be very difficult assess (e.g. self-confidence, adaptability, self-motivation, commitment, etc) and this is recognised as problematic by even the most enthusiastic advocates of employability. However, Yorke and Knight (2007: 168) argue that:

> in taking the line that self-efficacy and employability resist measurement (but not other forms of description), we are setting out a special case of the general position that we have taken, namely that there are many educational achievements that defy summative assessment, unless the resourcing is enormous – and then the act of measuring can destabilise what is being measured.

So the authors advocate the use of formative rather than summative assessment. They believe that formative assessment is important so students can learn from prior assignment work and are encouraged to take risks. Considerate feedback, say Knight and Yorke, should help build learner-confidence and sense of achievement. Biggs and Moore (1993) encourage the self-assessment of formative work and skills development so that students are encouraged to be more autonomous learners and learn from their own mistakes. Peer assessment is also important.

However formative assessment may not be so straightforward to deliver. Part of the problem, for many academics, is the time available for such formative assessment on short unitised courses, such as semester-length modules:

There is considerable evidence that semester modules are almost exclusively sum-
matively assessed and often the assessment is convenience assessment rather than
considered, suitable assessment to match programme objectives. Knight and
Yorke (2003b) argue that the best answer lies in looking at programme assessment
plans and moving away from the traditional concern with the individual course
or module. This is in keeping with what was said earlier about treating employability as, first and foremost, a programme issue (Harvey and Knight, 2003).

The briefing goes on to suggest that:

> in order to reduce clutter and 'task overload', it is a good idea to design modules
> to have a few 'target' outcomes that naturally call upon understanding and skil-
> ful practices that will not be directly assessed in that module. Such outcomes
> ought to make the exercise of understanding and skilfulness-in-practice a neces-
> sary condition for a student's success, even if the actual summative assessment
> does not specifically address them. These target outcomes need to be deter-
> mined in the light of the programme as a whole (or, perhaps, the 'core' elements
> of the programme).

The conclusion here is one of not side-stepping important assessment issues but
of accepting that summative assessment cannot possibly measure all valued outcomes of education. Indeed, one could argue that summative assessment can only
be used reliably in a limited range of circumstances to assess very small parts of
student's subject knowledge.

Conclusion

The final chapter of this book has drawn attention to some areas of employability which require further consideration. However, we hope it is clear that, while
not all the issues have been resolved, there is still considerable scope to embed
approaches which will enhance the employability of graduates. It is a vital aspect
of a student's entitlement at university and why many of them embark on their
courses in the first place.

Like it or not, employability is something that needs to be addressed and
there is clear evidence that many HEIs are embracing and embedding it in their
institutions and courses, albeit with varying degrees of enthusiasm. Even those
academics and sceptics who embrace more liberal views of what education is for
(and eschew what they perceive as the drive towards a market-driven model) can
also recognise the four main purposes of HE outlined by Robbins in 1963 (cited
in Lomas, 1997: 114):

   o to develop in students the necessary skills so that they could play their part in

the division of labour
- o to promote the general powers of the mind
- o to advance learning
- o and transmit a common culture and standards of citizenship.

The title of this book (and this chapter) posed the question *Enhancing Graduate Employability: can higher education deliver?* All the evidence presented here suggests the answer is a resounding 'Yes!' Employability is here to stay and the research being conducted on how best to embed it into a university education means that practices can only improve. Employability will not replace the fundamental focus of education: to develop the student's mind – rather it will compliment and perhaps even enhance this development process. This is good news for that most important of all HE stakeholders: the student.

Appendix 1

Aspects of employability (Yorke and Knight, 2006)

A   Personal Qualities
1 **Malleable self theory**: belief that attributes (e.g. intelligence) are not fixed and can be developed
2 **Self awareness**: awareness of own strengths and weaknesses, aims and values
3 **Self-confidence**: confidence in dealing with the challenges in employment and life
4 **Independence**: ability to work without supervision
5 **Emotional intelligence**: sensitivity to others' emotions and the effects they can have
6 **Adaptability**: ability to respond positively to changing circumstances and new challenges
7 **Stress tolerance**: ability to retain effectiveness under pressure
8 **Initiative**: ability to take action unprompted
9 **Willingness to learn**: commitment to ongoing learning to meet the needs of employment and life
10 **Reflectiveness**: the disposition to reflect evaluatively on the performance of oneself and others.

B   Core Skills
11 **Reading effectiveness**: the recognition and retention of key points
12 **Numeracy**: ability to use numbers at an appropriate level of accuracy
13 **Information retrieval**: ability to access different information sources
14 **Language skills**: possession of more than a single language
15 **Self-management**: ability to work in an efficient and structured manner
16 **Critical analysis**: ability to 'deconstruct' a problem or situation
17 **Creativity**: ability to be original or inventive and to apply lateral thinking
18 **Listening**: focused attention in which key points are recognised
19 **Written communication**: clear reports, letters, etc., written specifically for the reader

20 **Oral presentations**: clear and confident presentation of information to a group
21 **Explaining**: orally and in writing
22 **Global awareness**: in terms of both cultures and economics.

C   *Process Skills*

23 **Computer literacy**: ability to use a range of software
24 **Commercial awareness**: understanding of business issues and priorities
25 **Political sensitivity**: appreciates how organisations actually work and acts accordingly
26 **Ability to work cross-culturally**: both within and beyond UK
27 **Ethical sensitivity**: appreciates ethical aspects of employment and acts accordingly
28 **Prioritising**: ability to rank tasks according to importance
29 **Planning**: setting of achievable goals and structuring action
30 **Applying subject understanding**: use of disciplinary understanding from HE programme (e.g. marketing, finance, human resource management etc)
31 **Acting morally**: has a moral code and acts accordingly
32 **Coping with ambiguity and complexity**: ability to handle ambiguous and complex situations
33 **Problem-solving**: selection and use of appropriate methods to find solutions
34 **Influencing**: convincing others of the validity of one's point of view
35 **Arguing** for and/or justifying a point of view or a course of action
36 **Resolving conflict**: both intra-personally and in relationships with others
37 **Decision making**: choice of the best option from a range of alternatives
38 **Negotiating**: discussion to achieve mutually satisfactory resolution of contentious issues
39 **Teamwork**: can work constructively with others on a common task.

Source: Yorke, M. and Knight, P. T. (2006) *Embedding employability into the curriculum.* Learning and Employability Series One. York: HEA Enhancing Student Employability Co-ordination Team p 8

Appendix 2

Employability Audit

An Audit is a good way to initiate discussion and development on an issue. It enables you to make clear the range of activities which may contribute to the issue and the process can reassure colleagues that quite a lot of work may already be developed in the area. The process can also recognise local autonomy and priorities, within an institutional frame-work, and can:

- encourage development of a strategic plan to clarify how employability can be developed in relation to a particular discipline;
- identify how far and in what area development should take place;
- give recognition to existing activity which contributes effectively.

However an Audit also serves broader purposes:

- raising awareness by staff of practice in general and of the institution's plans;
- engaging a wider constituency within the academic community; and
- facilitating dialogue and development within and between teaching units.

The purpose of this audit is developmental, not simply to come up with an overall score for the course. It is designed to help teachers consider the content and design of a course with respect to the issue of employability and to see where they could improve the course to better address this issue.

The Employability Audit can be downloaded from the Centre for Bioscience website:

www.bioscience.heacademy.ac.uk/resources/audit.aspx

The audit can be changed to suit your requirements. All we ask is that you clearly acknowledge Centre for Bioscience as the originator. We would appreciate it if you would let us know that you are using the audit tool and the nature of any changes you have made as a result of your analysis.

Centre for Bioscience
The Higher Education Academy
Room 9.15 Worsley Building
University of Leeds, Leeds LS2 9JT
Tel / Fax: 0113 343 3001 / 5894
Email: heabioscience@leeds.ac.uk

Employability Audit

An Audit is a good way to initiate discussion and development on an issue. It enables you to make clear the range of activities which may contribute to the issue and the process can reassure colleagues that quite a lot of work may already be developed in the area. The process can also recognise local autonomy and priorities, within an institutional frame-work, and can:

- encourage development of a strategic plan to clarify how employability can be developed in relation to a particular discipline;
- identify how far and in what area development should take place;
- give recognition to existing activity which contributes effectively.

However an Audit also serves broader purposes:

- raising awareness by staff of practice in general and of the institution's plans;
- engaging a wider constituency within the academic community; and
- facilitating dialogue and development within and between teaching units.

The purpose of this audit is developmental, not simply to come up with an overall score for the course. It is designed to help teachers consider the content and design of a course with respect to the issue of employability and to see where they could improve the course to better address this issue.

The Employability Audit can be downloaded from the Centre for Bioscience website:

www.bioscience.heacademy.ac.uk/resources/audit.aspx

The audit can be changed to suit your requirements. All we ask is that you clearly acknowledge Centre for Bioscience as the originator. We would appreciate it if you would let us know that you are using the audit tool and the nature of any changes you have made as a result of your analysis.

Centre for Bioscience
The Higher Education Academy
Room 9.15 Worsley Building
University of Leeds, Leeds LS2
Tel / Fax: 0113 343 3001 / 58
Email: heabioscience@leeds.ac.uk

Last updated July 08

1. Graduate employment

	Score
Do academic staff know who actually employs your graduates?	
Has graduate employment destination data been circulated to academic staff within the last 2 years?	
Do current students know who employs graduates from this course?	
Do recent graduates visit to talk about their current jobs?	
Are students made aware of where they can obtain information on graduate destinations in employment?	
Are students aware at an early stage of the employment opportunities open to them?	

2. Career-path development

	Score
Are visitors giving research talks encouraged to reveal their own career paths?	
Are graduate career profiles available to students?	
Do recent graduates visit to talk about their career paths?	
Do more senior graduates visit to talk about their career paths?	
Are students explicitly taught career management skills?	

3. Relationships with employers

	Score
Have you made potential employers aware of the skills your students develop?	
Is your institution/unit on the list of favoured institutions with important employers?	
Do you know what employers perceive to be the strengths and weaknesses of your students?	
Do students have the opportunity to visit local employers?	
Do you have good communication with major employers of your graduates?	

Centre for Bioscience
www.bioscience.heacademy.ac.uk/resources/audit.aspx

3. Relationships with employers (cont.)

	Score
Do employers visit your unit to give talks about employment opportunities?	
Do employers attend any student final year project presentations?	
Do you know what skills, knowledge and attitudes your major employers see as becoming more important in the next 4 years?	

4. Options for work experience

	Score
Are work experience opportunities provided/encouraged during vacations?	
Are sandwich placements provided/encouraged as part of the course?	
Are overseas placements possible and encouraged for students?	
Are realistic simulations used to give experience of real work situations?	
Do some students carry out course project work in real settings with employers?	
Are work placements available in areas not involving your specific discipline?	
What proportion of students on your course have obtained work experience before graduation? (0=don't know; 1=<5%; 2=5 to 20%; 3=20 to 50%; 4=>50%)	
Are students on work placements supported by a process which encourages reflection and emphasises breadth of learning opportunities?	

5. Does your curriculum promote employability?

	Score
Do you know specifically what employers are looking for in graduates?	
Have employers reviewed your curriculum and provided feedback on its content?	
Are generic skills (e.g. communication, group working, IT) explicitly taught?	
Are generic skills assessed?	
Is there a skills matrix which is completed by each student?	

Centre for Bioscience
www.bioscience.heacademy.ac.uk/resources/audit.aspx

Last updated July 08

5. Does your curriculum promote employability? (cont.)

	Score
Are subject-specific skills taught and practiced?	
Are subject-specific skills assessed?	
Can you detect any of your students who are not numerate?	
Do you assess ability to write clear, concise, correct English?	
Are key skills and employability issues in the relevant QAA benchmarking statement incorporated in your curriculum?	
Do students have a choice of modules or choice of work areas within a module so they can tailor the content of their course to their perceived needs/interests?	
Are appropriate professional attitudes developed and discussed with students?	
Have you identified where work related learning activities take place in the course and are these made explicit to students?	
Have opportunities to increase work related learning in the course been identified and taken?	
Are all students given a basic grounding in ethics within the discipline field?	

6. Are students helped in obtaining and developing careers?

	Score
Is a 'Record of Achievement' maintained throughout the course?	
Is reflection on and review of achievements actively promoted within the course?	
Do students get help with producing/improving a CV?	
Do students get help with letters of application for employment?	
Is help with module choice available in each year?	

Centre for Bioscience
www.bioscience.heacademy.ac.uk/resources/audit.aspx

7. Extra-curricula activity

	Score
Is the contribution of extra-curricula activity to CV and skills development explained to students early in the course?	
Are extra-curricula activities and responsibilities recorded by your students?	
Are extra-curricula activities known to staff (e.g. personal tutors)?	
Are arrangements in place to encourage voluntary work by students?	

8. General

	Score
Is there an effective relationship between the course team and your Careers Service?	
Are students explicitly guided in the course to make contact with the Careers Service?	
Do you know the name of the Careers Adviser associated with your subject?	
Are your students encouraged to have confidence and high aspirations?	
Do staff generally have access to full information about a student's in course and extra-curricula performance (e.g. student's CV) when writing references?	
Have you considered employability in the context of widening participation?	
Have you considered employability in the context of disability?	
Have you considered employability in the context of ethnicity?	

Action Plan
Make a note of the resources you will need and whose help will be required.
1.

2.

3.

4.

Appendix 3   *Graduate skills valued by employers: summary table*

Harvey & Green (1994)	AGR (1995)	Reuters (1999)	Andrews & Higson (2007)	Archer and Davison (2008)
1 Willingness to learn	**Self-reliance skills**	**Intellectual skills**	Professionalism	Communication skills
2 Commitment	Self-awareness – purposeful, focused, self-belief, realistic	1 Assimilate/abstract information	Reliability	Team-working skills
3 Dependability/reliability	Proactivity – resourceful, drive, self-reliant	2 Identify key issues	Ability to cope with uncertainty	Integrity
4 Self-motivation	Willingness to learn – inquisitive, motivated, enthusiastic	3 Evaluate evidence	Ability to work under pressure	Intellectual ability
5 Team work	Self-promotion – positive, persistent, ambitious	4 Synthesise argument	Ability to plan and think strategically	Confidence
6 Communication skills – oral	Networking – initiator, relationship-builder, resourceful	5 Argue logically	Ability to communicate and interact with others, either in teams or through networking	Character/personality
7 Co-operation	Planning action – decision-maker, planner, able to prioritise	6 Put theory into practice	Good written and verbal communication skills	Planning & organisational skills
8 Communication skills- written	**People skills**	**Interpersonal skills**	ICT skills	Literacy (good writing skills)
9 Drive/energy	Team working – supportive, organised, co-ordinator, deliverer	1 Communicate effectively	Creativity and self-confidence	Numeracy (good with numbers)
10 Self-management	Interpersonal skills – listener, adviser, co-operative, assertive	2 Present ideas persuasively	Good self-management and time-management skills	Analysis & decision-making skills
11 Motivation	Oral communication – communicator, presenter, influencer	3 Work with others	Willingness to learn and accept responsibility	
12 Problem-solving ability	Leadership – motivator, energetic, visionary	4 Self-confidence		
13 Analytic ability	Customer orientation – friendly, caring, diplomatic	5 Compromise		
14 Flexibility	Foreign language – specific language skills	6 Flexibility		
15 Initiative		**Operational skills**		
16 Ability to precis		1 Problem-solving on own & in groups		
17 Logical argument		2 Self-reliance		
18 Adaptability (intellectual)		3 Common sense		
19 Numeracy		4 Interpret information – numerical, written, verbal		
20 Adaptability (organisational)		5 IT skills		
21 Ability to cope with pressure		6 Awareness of how businesses work		
22 Time management				
23 Rapid conceptualisation of issues				
24 Research skills				
25 Self-confidence				

General employment skills

Problem-solving – practical, logical, results orientated

Flexibility – versatile, willing, multi-skilled

Business acumen – entrepreneurial, competitive, risk taker

IT/computer literacy – office skills, keyboard skills, software packages

Numeracy – accurate, quick-thinker, methodical

Commitment – dedicated, trustworthy, conscientious

Specialist skills

Specific occupational skills – specialist relevant knowledge, eg languages, IT

Technical skills – e.g. journalism, engineering, accounting, sales

References and Links

Abramson, M. and Jones, P. (2001) Getting students off to a flying start: improving the retention of advanced GNVQ students entering higher education. *Widening Participation and Lifelong Learning* **3** (2) pp 34–37

AGCAS (2005) *Hospitality Sector.* Sector Briefings 2005. AGCAS and Graduate Prospects

AGCAS (2006) *Food and Drink Overview.* AGCAS and Prospects Report available at: http://www.prospects.ac.uk/cms/documents/Explore_job_sectors/Food_and_drink.pdf?id=12302

AGCAS (2007) *Hospitality Overview.* AGCAS and Prospects Report available at: http://www.prospects.ac.uk/cms/documents/Explore_job_sectors/Hospitality.pdf?id=3225

AGCAS (2007) *Sport and Leisure Overview.* AGCAS and Prospects Report available at: http://www.prospects.ac.uk/cms/documents/Explore_job_sectors/Sport_and_leisure.pdf?id=3212

AGR (1995) *Skills for Graduates in the 21st Century.* Cambridge: Association of Graduate Recruiters

AGR (2002) *Graduate Salaries and Vacancies Survey 2002.* Warwick, Association of Graduate Recruiters, January

AGR (2005) *Graduate employer survey.* Warwick, Association of Graduate Recruiters, Summer

AGR (2007) *Graduate Vacancies in UK set to increase for fourth consecutive year.* AGR Graduate Recruitment Survey Winter 2007 available at: www.agr.org.uk

AGR (2008) Graduate vacancies in UK set to increase for fourth consecutive year. *Education and Training* **49** (4)

Ainley, P. (1993) *Class and Skill: Changing Divisions of Knowledge and Labour.* London: Cassell

Allison, J., Harvey, C. and Nixon, I. (2002) Enhancing Employability: A long term strategic challenge. University of Newcastle. Available at http://www.heacademy.ac.uk/resources.asp?process=full_record&section=generic&id=459

Andrews, J. and Higson, H. (2007) *The MISLEM Project: Education, Employment and Graduate Employability Project Manual.* Aston Centre for Research into Higher Education

Archer, W. and Davison, J. (2008) *Graduate Employability: What do employers think and want?* The Council for Industry and Higher Education

Ashton, D. and Green, F. (1996) *Education, Training and the Global Economy.* Cheltenham, Edward Elgar

Association for Tourism in Higher Education (2007) *ATHE Report on Tourism Higher Education in the UK,* 2007

Atkins, M. (1999) Oven-ready and Self-basting: Taking Stock of Employability Skills. *Teaching in Higher Education* **4** (2) 267–80

Atlay, M and Harris, R. (2000) An Institutional Approach to Developing Students' 'Transferable' Skills. *Innovations in Education and Training International* **37** (1) pp 76–84

Baker, M. (2008) Students: Customers or learners? *BBC News.* Available at: http://newsvote.bbc.co.uk/mpapps/pagetools/print/news.bbc.co.uk/1/hi/education/746

Bandura, A. (1997) *Self-efficacy: The Exercise of Control.* New York: Freeman

BASES (2008) *A Guide to Careers in Sport and Exercise Sciences.* Available at: www.bases.org.uk

Beattie, I., Nixon, S. and Walker, C. (2008) From potential to achievement: enhancing students' value to employers. In Graves, S. and Maher, A. (eds) *Developing Graduate Employability Case Studies in Hospitality, Leisure, Sport and Tourism.* Newbury: Threshold Press

Becker, G. S. (1975) *Human Capital*. Chicago University Press, Chicago

Bekhradnia, B. (2005) *20 Years of Higher Education Policy in the United Kingdom: Looking Back 10 Years and Forward to the Next Decade*. CHERI, London

Biggs, J. (2003) *Teaching for Quality Learning at University* (2nd edn). Buckingham: SRHE and Open University Press

Biggs, J. B. & Moore, P. (1993) *The Process of Learning* (3rd edn). London: Prentice Hall

Bill, K. (2008) Entrepreneurship in sport. In Graves, S. and Maher, A. (eds) *Developing Graduate Employability Case Studies in Hospitality, Leisure, Sport and Tourism*. Newbury: Threshold Press

Blackwell, A. and Harvey, L. (1999) *Destinations and Reflections: The careers of art, craft and design students Executive Summary*. Centre for Research into Quality, Birmingham

Booth, A. (2001) Developing history students' skills in the transition to university. *Teaching in Higher Education* **6** (4) pp. 487–503

Boud, D. and Solomon, N. (eds) (2003) *Work Based Learning: A New Higher Education?* Buckingham: Open University Press

Bourner, T. and Ellerker, M. (1994) Sandwich placements: improving the learning experience – part 2. *Education and Training* **40** (6/7) pp. 288–95

Bowes, L. and Harvey, L. (1999) *The Impact of Sandwich Education on the Activities of Graduates Six Months Post-Graduation*. Centre for Research into Quality, Birmingham

Brennan, D. and Murphy, D. (2008) Using PDP to track, audit and evidence employability skills. In Graves, S. and Maher, A. (eds) *Developing Graduate Employability Case Studies in Hospitality, Leisure, Sport and Tourism*. Newbury: Threshold Press

Brennan, J. and Little, B. (1996) *A Review of Work-Based Learning in Higher Education*. Sheffield: DfEE

Brennan, J. and Tang, W. (2008) *The employment of UK graduates: comparisons with Europe*. REFLEX Report to HEFCE No 1, forthcoming. Bristol: HEFCE

Brown, P. (2001) A strategy for skill formation in Britain. In Coffield, F. (ed) *What Progress Are We Making With Lifelong Learning?* University of Newcastle Department of Education pp 111–26

Brown, P. and Hesketh, A. (2004) *The Mismanagement of Talent*. Oxford: Oxford University Press

Brown, P., Hesketh, A. and Williams, S. (2003) Employability in a Knowledge-driven Economy. *Journal of Education and Work* **16** (2) pp. 107–26

Brown, P. and Lauder, H. (1999) Education, Globalization and Economic Development. In Ahier, J. and Esland, G. (eds) *Education, Training and the Future of Work*. The Open University

Brown, P. and Lauder, H. (2001) *Capitalism and Social Progress: the future of society in a global economy*. London: Palgrave

Brynin, M. (2002) Graduate density, gender, and employment. *British Journal of Sociology* **53** (2) pp. 363–81

Brynner, J. (1998) Education for what? *Education and Training*. **40** (1) pp 4–5

Buswell, J. and Tomkins, A. (2008) Enhancing employability through critical reflective learning. In Graves, S. and Maher, A. (eds) *Developing Graduate Employability Case Studies in Hospitality, Leisure, Sport and Tourism*. Newbury: Threshold Press

Butcher, V. (2004) *The role of card sorts in employability learning*. The Higher Education Academy. Available at: http://www.heacademy.ac.uk/resources.asp?process=full_record&section=generic&id=459

Callender, C. and Wilkinson, D. (2003) *2002/03 Student Income and Expenditure Survey: Students' income, expenditure and debt and changes since 1998*. Research Report No 487, Department of Education and Skills, Nottingham

CBI (2008) *Taking Stock: CBI education and skills survey 2008*. Available at: www.cbi.org.uk

Centre for Employability Through the Humanities (CETH) details available at: http://www.uclan.ac.uk/facs/class/cfe/ceth/index.html

Centres for Excellence in Teaching and Learning (CETL) Projects details available at: http://www.heacademy.ac.uk/ourwork/networks/cetls

Centre for Research and Evaluation (2005) *Defining Employability.* Sheffield Hallam University. Available at: http://www.shu.ac.uk/research/cre/Employabilitydefiningemployability.htm

Centre for Research and Evaluation details available at: http://www.shu.ac.uk/research/cre/

CHME (2001) *Getting ahead: graduate careers in hospitality management.* HEFCE Report 01/30 May 2001

CIHE (2003) *The value of higher education.* London: CIHE

CIHE (2004) *Employability: Employer Perceptions of Subject Benchmark Statements.* available at: http://www.cihe-uk.com/docs/PUBS/forbes.pdf

CIHE (2005) *Work Based Learning; a consultation ... informing the debate.* The Council for Industry and Higher Education

CIHE (2006) *Student employability Profiles: A guide for higher education practitioners.* York: The Higher Education Academy

CIHE (2008) *Graduate Employability: What do employers think and want?* The Council for Industry and Higher Education

Clegg, S. (2004) Critical Readings: progress files and the production of the autonomous learner. *Teaching in Higher Education* **9** (3) pp. 287–98

Connon, J., Stevenson, A. and Cruickshank, S. (2005) *Enhancing Student Employability: Developing Successful Mentoring Partnerships.* 2005–6 Employability Enhancement Theme available at: http://www.enhancementthemes.ac.uk/themes/Employability/publications.asp

Curtis, P. (2005) End 'Social divide' in HE, says Rammell. *The Guardian* 16 November 2005

Dacre Pool, L. and Sewell, P. (2007) The key to employability: developing a practical model of graduate employability. *Education and Training* **49** (4) pp. 277–89

Danto, A. C. (1985) *Narration and Knowledge.* New York: Columbia University Press

Dearing, R. (1997) *The Dearing Report – National Committee of Inquiry into Higher Education.* National Report – Future Demands for higher education. HMSO, London

DfEE (1998) *'The Work Experience Bank' Students' Work: a study of the work experience of students.* DfEE

DIUS (2008) *Higher Education at Work: High Skills: High Value.* Available at: www.dius.gov.uk/consultations/con_0408_hlss.html

Dunne, E., Bennet, N. and Carre, C. (2000) Skill development in higher education and employment. In Coffield, F. (ed) *Differing Visions of a Learning Society.* Research findings Volume 1. The Policy Press & ESRC

Dunne, E. J. and Rawlins, M. (2000) Bridging the gap between industry and higher education: training academics to promote student teamwork. *Innovations in Education and Training International* **37** (4) pp 361–71

Dweck, C. S (1999) *Self-theories: their role in motivation, personality and development.* Philadelphia, PA: Psychology Press

Edwards, G. (2005) *Connecting PDP to Employer Needs and the World of Work.* York: Higher Education Academy

Elias, P. and Purcell, K. (2005 revised) *The earnings of graduates in their early careers. Graduate Careers Seven Years On.* Research Paper No. 5 IER Warwick/ESRU UWE

Elias, P. and Purcell, L. (2004) Is Mass Higher Education Working? Evidence from the Labour Market Experiences of Recent Graduates. *National Institute Economic Review* **190** (1) pp 60–74

Enhancing Graduate Employability (FDTL5) Project details at: www.enhancingemployability.org.uk

Entwhistle, N. (1996) Recent Research on student learning. In Tait, J. and Knight, P. (eds) *The Management of Independent Learning.* London: Kogan Page. pp. 97–112

Fallows, S. and Steven, C. (2000) Building employability skills into the higher education curriculum: a university-wide initiative. *Education and Training* 42 (2) pp. 75–83

Finegold, D. and Soskice, D. (1988) The Failure of Training in Britain: Analysis and Prescription. *Oxford Review of Economic Policy* (3) pp. 21–53

Frewin, A. (2004) Skills gap affects nearly one-third of hospitality and leisure businesses, *Caterer and Hotelkeeper* 10 November 2004

Fund for the Development of Teaching and Learning (FDTL) Projects details available at: http://www. heacademy.ac.uk/ourwork/networks/fdtl

Gifford, A. and Robertson, J. (2005) *Integrating Employment, PDP and Work-Based Learning into the Curriculum.* 2004–05 Employability Quality Enhancement Theme – Employability Roadshow. Available at: http://www.enhancementthemes.ac.uk/themes/Employability/publications.asp

Godfrey, H. (2005) *Effective Learning and Career Development PS22013.* 2004–05 Employability Quality Enhancement Theme – Employability Roadshow. Available at: http://www.enhancementthemes.ac.uk/themes/Employability/publications.asp

Goleman, D. (1996) *Emotional Intelligence.* London: Bloomsbury

Gough, D. A., Kirwan, D., Sutcliffe, S., Simpson, D. and Houghton, N. (2003) *A systemic map and synthesis review of the effectiveness of personal development planning for improving student learning.* London: The Evidence for Policy and Practice Information Co-ordinating Centre, Social Services Research Unit, Institute of Education, University of London

Haigh, M. J. and Kilmartin, M. P. (1999) Student Perception of the Development of Personal Transferable Skills. *Journal of Geography in Higher Education* 23 (2) pp. 195–206

Harris, M. (2001) *Developing Modern Higher Education Careers Services.* Report of the Review led by Sir Martin Harris, Vice-Chancellor, Manchester University. Department for Education and Employment, United Kingdom

Harvey, L. (2000a) An Employability Performance Indicator? *Perspectives* 4 (4) pp. 105–9

Harvey, L. (2000b) New realities: the relationship between higher education and employment. *Tertiary Education and Management* (6) pp. 3–17

Harvey, L. (2001) Defining and Measuring Employability. *Quality in Higher Education* 7 (2) pp. 97–109

Harvey, L. (2003) *Transitions from higher education to work.* York: ESECT/LTSN. February

Harvey, L. (2004) On Employability. The Higher Education Academy. Available at http://www.palatine. ac.uk/files/emp/1236.pdf

Harvey, L., Burrows, A. and Green, D. (1992) *Someone Who Can Make an Impression. Report of the employers' survey of qualities of higher education graduates.* Birmingham, QHE

Harvey, L., Geall, V. and Moon, S. with Aston, J., Bowes, L. and Blackwell, A. (1998) *Work Experience: Expanding opportunities for undergraduates.* Centre for Research into Quality (CRQ) Birmingham

Harvey, L. and Green, D. (1994) *Employer satisfaction: summary.* QHE Project. University of Central England

Harvey, L. and Knight, P. (2003) *Briefings on Employability: Helping departments to develop employ-ability.* ESECT and LTSN available at: http://www.heacademy.ac.uk/resources/detail/Employability/employability282?i=academyYork

Harvey, L., Locke, W. and Morey, A. (2002) *Enhancing Employability, Recognising Diversity.* Universities UK and Careers Service Unit, London

Harvey, L. and Morey, A. (2002) *Enhancing employability, recognising diversity: making links between higher education and the world of work.* Universities UK and CSU

Harvey, L., Moon, S., Geall, V. with Bower, R. (1997) *Graduates' Work: Organisational Change and Students' Attributes.* Birmingham: CRQ and AGR

HE Courses-Careers (2008) *Studying Sport and Exercise Science in the UK.* Sandringham Publishing Ltd, available at: http://www.hecourses-careers.com/sports.htm

HEFCE (2006) *Recurrent Grants for 2006–7.* Available at: http://www.hefce. ac.uk/pubs/hefce/2006/06_08/06_08.pdf

Hills, J., Barron, E., Freeman, P., Adey, M., Robertson, G. and Murphy, R. (2003) *Dine Out on Work Related Learning.* Good Practice Guide to the Implementation of Work Related Learning in Agriculture, Forestry, Environment and Organismal Bioscience. University of Newcastle upon Tyne

Hingley, V. (2008) Developing employability skills through employer engagement in Foundation degrees. In Graves, S. and Maher, A. (eds) *Developing Graduate Employability Case Studies in Hospitality, Leisure, Sport and Tourism.* Newbury: Threshold Press

Hirst, P. (1965) Liberal Education and the Nature of Knowledge. In Archambault, R. (ed) *Philosophical Analysis and Education.* London: Routledge

Hospitality, Leisure, Sport and Tourism Subject Network details available at: http://www.heacademy. ac.uk/hlst

Hospitality Training Foundation (2000) *Labour Market Review*

Ineson, E. (2005) *Industry-Education Links to Promote Hospitality and Tourism Management Applied Research and Consultancy Skills.* Case study available at: http://www.heacademy. ac.uk/hlst/resources/employability_resources

ISPAL (2008) *A career in sport, parks and leisure.* Available at: http://www.ispal.org.uk/info_hub. cfm?page=careers

Jameson, S. (2008) International hospitality students' development of employability skills in the placement module. In Graves, S. and Maher, A. (eds) *Developing Graduate Employability Case Studies in Hospitality, Leisure, Sport and Tourism.* Newbury: Threshold Press

Jameson, S. and Walmsley, A. (2006) *A Review of Hospitality Management Education in the UK 2006.* Council for Hospitality Management Education

Jameson, S., Walmsley, A. and Ball, S. (CHME) (2005) *A Review of Hospitality Management Education in the UK.* Council for Hospitality Management Education

Keep, E. (2003) No Problem. *The Guardian* 16 December 2003

Keep, E. and Mayhew, K. (1996) Economic demand for higher education – a sound foundation for further expansion? *Higher Education Quarterly* 50 (2) pp. 89–109

Keep, E. and Mayhew, K. (1999) The assessment of knowledge, skills and competitiveness. *Oxford Review of Economic Policy* 15 (1) pp. 1–15

Keep, E. (2002) The English Vocational Education and Training Policy Debate – Fragile 'Technologies' or Opening the 'Black Box': two competing visions of where we go next. *Journal of Education and Work* 15 (4) pp. 457–79

King, M. (2007) *Workforce development: how much engagement do employers have with higher education? A review of the evidence on employer demand.* The Council for Industry and Higher Education

Kingston, B. (2003) Top ten favourites retain poll positions. *The Times Higher Education Supplement* 10 October 2003 p 6

Knight, P. (2001) Employability and Assessment. Skills *plus* – a paper prepared for the fourth colloquium 3 October 2001

Knight, P. and Yorke, M. (2000) *Skills Plus: Tuning the undergraduate curriculum.* Skills *Plus* Project Report

Knight, P. and Yorke, M. (2003) *Assessment, Learning and Employability.* Maidenhead: Open University Press

Knight, P. and Yorke, M. (2004) *Learning, Curriculum and Employability in Higher Education.* London: RoutledgeFalmer

Knight, P. T. and Yorke, M., (2006) Employability: judging and communicating achievements. *Learning and Employability Series One.* York: HEA – Enhancing Student Employability Co-ordination Team

Lees, D. (2002) *Graduate Employability – literature review.* LTSN Generic Centre, October

Leitch Review of Skills (2006) *Prosperity for All in the Global Economy – World Class Skills.* HMSO, London

Little, B. (2001) Reading between the lines of graduate employment. *Quality in Higher Education* 7 (2) pp 121–29

Little, B. (2004) Employability and work-based learning. *Learning and Employability Series One.* ESECT: The Higher Education Academy

Little, B. and Harvey, L. (2006) *Learning Through Work Placements and Beyond.* HESCU and the Higher Education Academy's Work Placement Organisation Forum

Little, Brenda and Harvey, Lee (2007) *UK work placements: a choice too far? Tertiary Education and Management* 13 (3) pp. 227–45

Little, B., Moon, S., Pierce, D., Harvey, L. and Marlow-Hayne, N. (2001) *Nature and Extent of Undergraduates' Work Experience.* CIHE/DFES, London

Little, B. and contributors (2003) International Perspectives on Employability. *The Perspectives Series on Employability.* ESECT and LTSN Generic Centre available at: http://www.palatine.ac.uk/files/emp/1260.pdf

Litteljohn, D. and Morrison, J. (1997) *Hospitality Management Education Report.* Council for Hospitality Management Education

Litteljohn, D. and Watson, S. (2004) Developing Graduate Managers for Hospitality and Tourism. *International Journal of Contemporary Hospitality Management* 16 (7) pp. 408–14

Lomas, L. (1997) The decline of liberal education and the emergence of a new model of education and training. *Education and Training* 39 (3) pp 111–14

LTSN (2002) *Graduate Employability.* Briefings for Senior Managers in Higher Education. LTSN Generic Centre Circular 5

LTSN (2003) *Guide for Busy Academics 3: Using Personal Development Planning to help students gain employment.* LTSN Generic Centre. Available at: http://www.heacademy.ac.uk/resources/detail/SNAS/snas_711?i=academyYork

LTSN (2005) *Guide for Busy Academics No 1: Personal Development Planning* Available at: http://www.heacademy.ac.uk/resources/detail/id66_guide_for_busy_academics_no1

Macfarlane-Dick, D. and Roy, A. (2006) *Enhancing Student Employability: Innovative Projects from across the Curriculum.* Quality Assurance Agency for Higher Education

Maher, A. (2004) Oven-ready and Self-basting? Taking stock of employability skills. *LINK 11.* Higher Education Academy Network for Hospitality, Leisure, Sport and Tourism

Maher, A. and Nield, K. (2005) Enhancing Student Employability: Higher Education and Workforce Development. Ninth Quality in Higher Education International Seminar in collaboration with ESECT and *The Independent.* Birmingham, January 27–28 2005

Martin, E. and McCabe, S. (2008) Embedding employability in postgraduate hospitality and tourism courses through work placement. In Graves, S. and Maher, A. (eds) *Developing Graduate Employability Case Studies in Hospitality, Leisure, Sport and Tourism.* Newbury: Threshold Press

Mason, G. (1999) *The Labour Market for Engineering, Science and IT Graduates: Are There Mismatches Between Supply and Demand?* Suffolk, DfEE

Mason, G. (2002) High skills utilisation under mass higher education: graduate employment in service industries in Britain. *Journal of Education and Work* 15 (4) pp. 427–56

McDury, J. and Alterio, M. (2003) *Learning through Storytelling in Higher Education: Using Reflection and Experience to Improve Learning.* London: Kogan Page

McNair, S. (2003) *Employability in Higher Education.* LTSN Generic Centre/University of Surrey

Medhat, S. (2003) A new beginning for a strained relationship. *Times Higher Education Supplement* 23 January 2003

Moreland, N. (2005) *Work-related Learning in Higher Education*. Learning and Employability Series Two. York: ESECT and the Higher Education Academy

National Employer Skills Survey (2007) Available at: http://researchtools.lsc.gov.uk/ness/home/home.asp

National Teaching Fellowship Scheme (NTFS) Project strand details available at: http://www.heacademy.ac.uk/ourwork/professional/ntfs/projects

Nixon, I., Smith, K., Stafford, R. and Camm, S. (2006) *Work-based learning: illuminating the higher education landscape*. York: The Higher Education Academy

Payne, J. (2000) All things to all people: changing perceptions of 'skill' among Britain's policy makers since the 1950s and their implications. *Skope Research Papers* No. 1. Oxford and Warwick

Pedagogy for Employability Group (2004) *Pedagogy for employability*. Learning and Employability Series. ESECT: The Higher Education Academy

People 1st (2006) *The hospitality, leisure, travel and tourism sector key facts and figures*. Available at: www.people1st.co.uk/research

Prospects (2003) *The impact of higher education on employment prospects and earnings*. Available at: http://prospects.ac.uk/cms/ShowPage/Home_page/Labour_market_information/

Purcell, K. and Elias, P. (2004) *Seven Years On: Graduate Careers in a Changing Labour Market – Short Report*. HECSU, ESRC, Warwick IER and ESRU

Purcell, K., Elias, P. and Wilton, N. (2003) *Researching Graduate Careers Seven Years On*. Research paper No. 3. ESRC and HECSU

Purcell, K., Elias, P., Davies, R. and Wilton, N. (2005) *The Class of '99: Graduate careers four years after graduation*. London: DfES

QAA (2001) *Section 8: Code of Practice for Careers Education, Information and Guidance*. In QAA Code of practice for the assurance of academic quality and standards in higher education. Available at: http://www.qaa.ac.uk/academicinfrastructure/codeofpractice/section8/default.asp

QAA (2008) *QAA Subject Benchmarks for Hospitality, Leisure, Sport and Tourism*. Available at: http://www.qaa.ac.uk/academicinfrastructure/benchmark/statements/HLST08.pdf

Ramsden, P. (2007) Inspiring tomorrow's students. *Academy Exchange* (7) Winter, 2007

Raybould, M and Wilkins, H. (2005) Over qualified and under experienced: Turning graduates into hospitality managers. *International Journal of Contemporary Hospitality Management* **17** (3) pp. 203–16

Reuters (1999) *Developing Workplace Skills*. Reuters Foundation

Robbins, L. (Chairman) (1963) *Higher Education*. Report to the Committee appointed by the Prime Minister under the chairmanship of Lord Robbins, 1961–63. HMSO, London

Ross, J. (2007) *Retaining Hospitality Graduates*. 4Hoteliers. Available at: http://www.4hoteliers.com/4hots_fshw.php?mwi=2257

Rotter, J. B. (1966) Generalised expectancies for internal versus external control of reinforcement. *Psychology Monographs* (80) pp. 1–28

Rust, C. (2002) The Impact of Assessment on Student Learning. *Active Learning in Higher Education* **3** (2) pp. 145–58

Sanderson, M. (1993) Vocational and Liberal Education: A Historian's View. *European Journal of Education* **28** (2) pp. 189–96

Scottish Enhancement Theme (2004/5) details available at: http://www.enhancementthemes.ac.uk/themes/Employability/default.asp

Sheehan, C. and Waghorn, L. (2008) Enhancing employability through work-based assessment. In Graves, S. and Maher, A. (eds) *Developing Graduate Employability Case Studies in Hospitality, Leisure, Sport and Tourism*. Newbury: Threshold Press

Shelley, S. (2005) *Working in Universities: The Realities from Porter to Professor*. Glasgow: Humming Earth

Smith, J., McKnight, A. and Naylor, R. A. (2000) Graduate Employability: Policy and Performance in Higher Education in the UK. *Economic Journal* (110) F382–F411

Snape, R. (2008) Personal Development Planning in the delivery and assessment of graduate employability skills. In Graves, S. and Maher, A. (eds) *Developing Graduate Employability Case Studies in Hospitality, Leisure, Sport and Tourism*. Newbury: Threshold Press

Stephenson, J. (2001) Ensuring a holistic approach to work-based learning: the capability envelope. In Boud, D. and Solomon, N. (eds) *Work-based learning: a new higher education?* Buckingham: SRHE and Open University Press pp. 86–102

Stephenson, J. and Yorke, M. (1998) Creating the conditions for the development of capability. In Stephenson, J. and Yorke, M. (eds) *Capability and Quality in Higher Education*. London: Kogan Page pp. 193–225

Sternberg, R. J. (1997) *Successful Intelligence: how practical and creative intelligence determine success in life*. New York: Plume

Sternberg, R. J. and Grigorenko, E. L. (2000) Practical Intelligence and its development. In Bar-On, R. and Parker, J. D. A. (eds) *The handbook of emotional intelligence: Theory, development, assessment, and application at home, school and in the workplace*. San Francisco, CA: Jossey-Bass pp. 215–43

Tapper, E. and Salter, B. (1995) The Changing Idea of University Autonomy. *Studies in Higher Education* 20 (1) pp. 59–72

UCAS (2008) Universities and Colleges Admissions Service *Course Search 2009* available at: http://www.ucas.ac.uk/students/coursesearch/coursesearch2009/

Universities UK (2007) *Beyond the Honours Degree Classification: Burgess Group Final Report*. Available at http://bookshop.universitiesuk.ac.uk/downloads/Burgess_final.pdf

Ward, R. and contributors (2006) *Personal development planning and employability*. Learning and Employability Series Two. ESECT: Higher Education Academy

Whittaker, C. (2008) Employability enhancement for new students approaching a work-experience year. In Graves, S. and Maher, A. (eds) *Developing Graduate Employability Case Studies in Hospitality, Leisure, Sport and Tourism*. Newbury: Threshold Press

Wright, W. A. and Knight, P. T. with Pomerleau, N. (2000) Portfolio People: teaching and learning dossiers and the future of higher education. *Innovative Higher Education* 24 (2) pp 89–102

Yorke, M. (2003) *Briefings on Employability 4: Encouraging the Development of Employability*. York: ESECT

Yorke, M. (2004) *Employability in higher education: what it is – what it is not*. Learning and Employability Series. ESECT: LTSN Generic Centre

Yorke, M. (2006) Employability and higher education: what it is – what it is not, *Learning and Employability Series One*. York: HEA – Enhancing Student Employability Co-ordination Team

Yorke, M and Knight, P. (2002) *Employability through the curriculum*. Skills Plus: Tuning the Undergraduate Curriculum. June 2002 edition

Yorke, M. and Knight, P. (2003) *The Undergraduate Curriculum and Employability*. The Perspectives Series of Employability Briefings. ESECT and LTSN Generic Centre

Yorke, M. and Knight, P. T. (2006) Embedding employability into the curriculum, *Learning and Employability Series One*. York: HEA – Enhancing Student Employability Co-ordination Team

Yorke, M. and Knight, P. (2007) Evidence-informed pedagogy and the enhancement of student employability. *Teaching in Higher Education* 12 (2) pp. 157–70

Index